THE COLLINS BOOK OF
LOVE POEMS

The Collins Book of

LOVE POEMS

CHOSEN BY AMANDA McCARDIE

with wood engravings by Kathleen Lindsley

*

COLLINS
8 Grafton Street London W1
1990

William Collins Sons & Co.
London · Glasgow · Sydney · Auckland
Toronto · Johannesburg

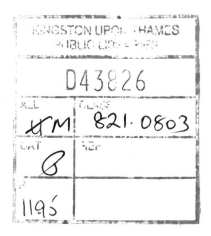
British Library CIP data is available on request

ISBN 0 00 223728 8

First published 1990
© this selection William Collins Sons & Co. 1990

Photoset in Itek Palatino by
Ace Filmsetting Ltd, Frome, Somerset
Made and printed in Great Britain by
T.J. Press (Padstow) Ltd, Padstow, Cornwall

Contents

Acknowledgements

The publishers gratefully acknowledge the following for permission to reproduce copyright poems in this book: John Arden for his poem 'I'll Make My Love a Breast of Glass'; Jonathan Cape Ltd on behalf of the Executors of the James Joyce Estate for 'O sweetheart, hear you' (XVIII) and 'I Hear an Army' from *Chamber Music* by James Joyce; Jonathan Cape Ltd on behalf of the Estate of Robert Frost for 'The Silken Tent' from *The Poetry of Robert Frost*, ed. Edward Connery Lathem; Rosica Colin Ltd on behalf of the Estate of Richard Aldington for 'Images' from *Complete Poems* by Richard Aldington; Collins Publishers for 'A Forge, and a Scythe' from *In A Marine Light* by Raymond Carver; Faber & Faber Ltd for 'Warm are the still and lucky miles' and 'Lullaby' from *Collected Poems* by W.H. Auden, for 'La Figlia che Piange' from *Collected Poems 1909–1962* by T.S. Eliot, for 'Glanmore Sonnets: X' and 'Homecomings' from *Field Work* by Seamus Heaney, for 'Song' from *The Hawk in the Rain* by Ted Hughes, for 'An Arundel Tomb' from *The Whitsun Weddings* by Philip Larkin, for 'Will Not Come Back' (Volveran) from *Notebook* by Robert Lowell, for Parts I and II of 'Trilogy For X' from *The Collected Poems of Louis MacNeice*, for 'The Confirmation' and 'In Love for Long' from *The Collected Poems of Edwin Muir*, for 'I Knew a Woman' from *The Collected Poems of Theodore Roethke*, and for 'Ice (Vienna): For Muriel' and 'The Room Above the Square' from *Collected Poems* by Stephen Spender; Grafton Books, a division of the Collins Publishing Group, for 'may i feel he said' from *Complete Poems: Vol. I* by e.e. cummings; Houghton Mifflin Company (Boston) for 'Not Marble Nor the Gilded Monuments' from *New and Collected Poems 1917–1982* by Archibald MacLeish, copyright © 1985 by the Estate of Archibald MacLeish; David Higham Associates Ltd for 'Winter Love' from *Collected Poems* by Elizabeth Jennings (Macmillan) and 'By the Lake' from *Collected Poems* by Edith Sitwell (Carcanet); Olwyn Hughes for 'Love Letter' from *Collected Poems* by Sylvia Plath (Faber & Faber Ltd), copyright © 1971 and 1981 by Ted Hughes; Laurence Pollinger Ltd on behalf of Alfred A. Knopf/Random House, Inc. for 'Piazza Piece' from *Selected Poems* by John Crowe Ransom (Methuen London Ltd); London Management for 'At the Dark Hour' from *The Fern on the Rock* by Paul Dehn; James MacGibbon, executor of the Stevie Smith Estate, for 'To the Tune of Coventry Carol' from *The Collected Poems of Stevie Smith* (Penguin Modern Classics); John Murray (Publishers) Ltd for 'Myfanwy' from *John Betjeman: Collected Poems*; Oxford University Press Inc. (New York) for 'Annihilation' from *Collected Poems* (second edition) by Conrad Aiken, copyright © 1953, 1970 by Conrad Aiken; Sebastian Peake and the Mervyn Peake Estate for 'Maeve' by Mervyn Peake; Kathleen Raine for 'Envoi' from *Collected Poems* by Kathleen Raine (Unwin Hyman Ltd); Random Century Ltd for 'I Am a Lamp that is Out' from *Collected Poems* by Frances Cornford; George T. Sassoon for 'Lovers' and 'What you are' from *Selected Poems* by Siegfried Sassoon; Martin Secker & Warburg for 'Raspberries' from *The Man I Killed* by Laurence Lerner; Louis Simpson for 'As Birds are Fitted to the Boughs' from *Selected Poems* by Louis Simpson (Oxford University Press); The University Press of New England for 'The Custom of the World' from *A Dream of Governors* by Louis Simpson, copyright © 1955 by Louis Simpson; Unwin Hyman Ltd for 'Goodbye', from *Ha! Ha! Among the Trumpets*, and 'Postscript: For Gweno', from *Raider's Dawn*, both by Alun Lewis; A.P. Watt Ltd on behalf of the Executors of the Estate of Robert Graves for 'Symptoms of Love', 'She Tells her Love While Half Asleep', 'Love Without Hope', and 'The Window Sill' from *Collected Poems* by Robert Graves (Cassell & Co Ltd); A.P. Watt Ltd on behalf of the Wodehouse Trust No. 3 for 'The Gourmet's Love-Song' by P.G. Wodehouse. Every effort has been made to contact the copyright holders of poems included in this book. In the instances where this has proved impossible, we offer our apologies to those concerned.

Love's
Birthday

*

'And now good morrow to our waking souls'

He Wishes For the Cloths
of Heaven

Had I the heavens' embroidered cloths,
Enwrought with golden and silver light,
The blue and the dim and the dark cloths
Of night and light and the half-light,
I would spread the cloths under your feet:
But I, being poor, have only my dreams;
I have spread my dreams under your feet;
Tread softly because you tread on my dreams.

W. B. YEATS

3

Love Without Hope

Love without hope, as when the young bird-catcher
Swept off his tall hat to the Squire's own daughter,
So let the imprisoned larks escape and fly
Singing about her head, as she rode by.

ROBERT GRAVES

To ————

One word is too often profaned
    For me to profane it;
One feeling too falsely disdained
    For thee to disdain it;
One hope is too like despair
    For prudence to smother;
And pity from thee more dear
    Than that from another.

I can give not what men call love:
    But wilt thou accept not
The worship the heart lifts above
    And the heavens reject not,
The desire of the moth for the star,
    Of the night for the morrow,
The devotion to something afar
    From the sphere of our sorrow?

PERCY BYSSHE SHELLEY

If I were loved

If I were loved, as I desire to be,
What is there in the great sphere of the earth,
And range of evil between death and birth,
That I should fear – if I were loved by thee?
All the inner, all the outer world of pain
Clear Love would pierce and cleave, if thou wert mine,
As I have heard that, somewhere in the main,
Fresh-water springs come up through bitter brine.
'Twere joy, not fear, claspt hand-in-hand with thee,
To wait for death – mute – careless of all ills,
Apart upon a mountain, tho' the surge
Of some new deluge from a thousand hills
Flung leagues of roaring foam into the gorge
Below us, as far on as eye could see.

ALFRED, LORD TENNYSON

Awake, my heart

Awake, my heart, to be loved, awake, awake!
The darkness silvers away, the morn doth break,
It leaps in the sky: unrisen lustres slake
The o'ertaken moon. Awake, O heart, awake!

She too that loveth awaketh and hopes for thee;
Her eyes already have sped the shades that flee,
Already they watch the path thy feet shall take:
Awake, O heart, to be loved, awake, awake!

And if thou tarry from her, – if this could be, –
She cometh herself, O heart, to be loved, to thee;
For thee would unashamèd herself forsake:
Awake to be loved, my heart, awake, awake!

Awake, the land is scattered with light, and see,
Uncanopied sleep is flying from field and tree:
And blossoming boughs of April in laughter shake;
Awake, O heart, to be loved, awake, awake!

Lo all things wake and tarry and look for thee:
She looketh and saith, 'O sun, now bring him to me.
Come more adored, O adored, for his coming's sake,
And awake my heart to be loved: awake, awake!'

ROBERT BRIDGES

7

Romance

I will make you brooches and toys for your delight
Of bird-song at morning and star-shine at night.
I will make a palace fit for you and me,
Of green days in forests and blue days at sea.

I will make my kitchen, and you shall keep your room,
Where white flows the river and bright blows the broom,
And you shall wash your linen and keep your body white
In rainfall at morning and dewfall at night.

And this shall be for music when no one else is near,
The fine song for singing, the rare song to hear!
That only I remember, that only you admire,
Of the broad road that stretches and the roadside fire.

ROBERT LOUIS STEVENSON

A Birthday

My heart is like a singing bird
    Whose nest is in a watered shoot;
My heart is like an apple-tree
    Whose boughs are bent with thickest fruit.
My heart is like a rainbow shell
    That paddles in a halcyon sea;
My heart is gladder than all these
    Because my love is come to me.

Raise me a dais of silk and down;
    Hang it with vair and purple dyes;
Carve it in doves and pomegranates,
    And peacocks with a hundred eyes;
Work it in gold and silver grapes,
    In leaves and silver fleurs-de-lys;
Because the birthday of my life
    Is come, my love is come to me.

CHRISTINA ROSSETTI

9

First Love

I ne'er was struck before that hour
  With love so sudden and so sweet.
Her face it bloomed like a sweet flower
  And stole my heart away complete.
My face turned pale as deadly pale,
  My legs refused to walk away,
And when she looked 'what could I ail?'
  My life and all seemed turned to clay.

And then my blood rushed to my face
  And took my sight away.
The trees and bushes round the place
  Seemed midnight at noonday.
I could not see a single thing,
  Words from my eyes did start;
They spoke as chords do from the string
  And blood burnt round my heart.

Are flowers the winter's choice?
  Is love's bed always snow?
She seemed to hear my silent voice
  And love's appeal to know.
I never saw so sweet a face
  As that I stood before:
My heart has left its dwelling-place
  And can return no more.

JOHN CLARE

The Mower to the Glow-Worms

Ye living lamps, by whose dear light
The nightingale does sit so late
And studying all the summer night,
Her matchless songs does meditate;

Ye country comets, that portend
No war, nor prince's funeral,
Shining unto no higher end
Than to presage the grasses' fall;

Ye glow-worms, whose officious flame
To wandering mowers shows the way,
That in the night have lost their aim,
And after foolish fires do stray;

Your courteous lights in vain you waste,
Since Juliana here is come,
For she my mind hath so displaced
That I shall never find my home.

ANDREW MARVELL

Love Letter

Not easy to state the change you made.
If I'm alive now, then I was dead,
Though, like a stone, unbothered by it,
Staying put according to habit.
You didn't just toe me an inch, no –
Nor leave me to set my small bald eye
Skyward again, without hope, of course,
Of apprehending blueness, or stars.

That wasn't it. I slept, say: a snake
Masked among black rocks as a black rock
In the white hiatus of winter –
Like my neighbors, taking no pleasure
In the million perfectly-chiseled
Cheeks alighting each moment to melt
My cheek of basalt. They turned to tears,
Angels weeping over dull natures,
But didn't convince me. Those tears froze.
Each dead head had a visor of ice.

And I slept on like a bent finger.
The first thing I saw was sheer air
And the locked drops rising in a dew
Limpid as spirits. Many stones lay
Dense and expressionless round about.
I didn't know what to make of it.
I shone, mica-scaled, and unfolded
To pour myself out like a fluid
Among bird feet and the stems of plants.
I wasn't fooled. I knew you at once.

Tree and stone glittered, without shadows.
My finger-length grew lucent as glass.
I started to bud like a March twig:
An arm and a leg, an arm, a leg.
From stone to cloud, so I ascended.
Now I resemble a sort of god
Floating through the air in my soul-shift
Pure as a pane of ice. It's a gift.

SYLVIA PLATH

A Red, Red Rose

O, my luve's like a red, red rose,
    That's newly sprung in June;
O, my luve's like the melodie
    That's sweetly play'd in tune.

As fair art thou, my bonnie lass,
    So deep in luve am I;
And I will luve thee still, my dear,
    Till a' the seas gang dry –

Till a' the seas gang dry, my dear,
    And the rocks melt wi' the sun;
I will luve thee still, my dear,
    While the sands of life shall run.

And fare thee weel, my only luve!
    And fare thee weel a while!
And I will come again, my luve,
    Tho' it were ten thousand mile.

ROBERT BURNS

From the Fourth of
Ten Lyric Pieces
in Celebration of Charis

Have you seen but a bright lily grow
Before rude hands have touched it?
Have you marked but the fall o' the snow
Before the soil hath smutched it?
Have you felt the wool of the beaver,
    Or swan's down ever?
Or have smelt o' the bud o' the brier,
    Or the nard in the fire?
Or have tasted the bag of the bee?
O so white, O so soft, O so sweet is she!

BEN JONSON

15

Myfanwy

Kind o'er the *kinderbank* leans my Myfanwy,
    White o'er the play-pen the sheen of her dress,
Fresh from the bathroom and soft in the nursery
    Soap-scented fingers I long to caress.

Were you a prefect and head of your dormit'ry?
    Were you a hockey girl, tennis or gym?
Who was your favourite? Who had a crush on you?
    Which were the baths where they taught you to swim?

Smooth down the Avenue glitters the bicycle,
    Black-stockinged legs under navy-blue serge,
Home and Colonial, Star, International,
    Balancing bicycle leant on the verge.

Trace me your wheel-tracks, you fortunate bicycle,
    Out of the shopping and into the dark.
Back down the Avenue, back to the pottingshed,
    Back to the house on the fringe of the park.

Golden the light on the locks of Myfanwy,
    Golden the light on the book on her knee,
Finger-marked pages of Rackham's Hans Andersen.
    Time for the children to come down to tea.

Oh! Fuller's angel-cake, Robertson's marmalade,
    Liberty lampshade, come, shine on us all.
My! what a spread for the friends of Myfanwy
    Some in the alcove and some in the hall.

Then what sardines in the half-lighted passages!
    Locking of fingers in long hide-and-seek.
You will protect me, my silken Myfanwy,
    Ringleader, tom-boy, and chum to the weak.

SIR JOHN BETJEMAN

16

What you are

What you are I cannot say;
Only this I know full well –
When I touched your face to-day
Drifts of blossom flushed and fell.

Whence you came I cannot tell;
Only – with your joy you start
Chime on chime from bell on bell
In the cloisters of my heart.

SIEGFRIED SASSOON

The Good Morrow

I wonder by my troth, what thou and I
Did, till we loved? were we not weaned till then,
But sucked on country pleasures, childishly?
Or snorted we in the seven sleepers' den?
'Twas so; but this, all pleasures fancies be.
If ever any beauty I did see,
Which I desired, and got, 'twas but a dream of thee.

And now good morrow to our waking souls,
Which watch not one another out of fear;
For love, all love of other sights controls,
And makes one little room, an everywhere.
Let sea-discoverers to new worlds have gone,
Let maps to others, worlds on worlds have shown,
Let us possess one world, each hath one, and is one.

My face in thine eye, thine in mine appears,
And true plain hearts do in the faces rest,
Where can we find two better hemispheres
Without sharp north, without declining west?
What ever dies, was not mixed equally;
If our two loves be one, or thou and I
Love so alike that none do slacken, none can die.

JOHN DONNE

The First Day

I wish I could remember the first day,
　　First hour, first moment of your meeting me;
　　If bright or dim the season, it might be
Summer or winter for aught I can say.
So unrecorded did it slip away,
　　So blind was I to see and to foresee,
　　So dull to mark the budding of my tree
That would not blossom yet for many a May.
If only I could recollect it! Such
　　A day of days! I let it come and go
　　As traceless as a thaw of bygone snow.
It seemed to mean so little, meant so much!
If only now I could recall that touch,
　　First touch of hand in hand! – Did one but know!

CHRISTINA ROSSETTI

Love's Passion

*

'My love is like to ice and I to fire'

21

The Voice from the Well

Fair maiden, white and red,
Comb me smooth, and stroke my head;
And thou shalt have some cockle bread.
Gently dip, but not too deep,
For fear thou make the golden beard to weep.
Fair maid, white and red,
Comb me smooth, and stroke my head;
And every hair a sheave shall be,
And every sheave a golden tree.

GEORGE PEELE

Delight in Disorder

A sweet disorder in the dress
Kindles in clothes a wantonness:
A lawn about the shoulders thrown
Into a fine distraction:
An erring lace, which here and there
Enthrals the crimson stomacher:
A cuff neglectful, and thereby
Ribbands to flow confusedly:
A winning wave, deserving note,
In the tempestuous petticoat:
A careless shoe-string, in whose tie
I see a wild civility:
Do more bewitch me than when art
Is too precise in every part.

Upon Julia's Voice

So smooth, so sweet, so silvery, is thy voice
As, could they hear, the damned would make no noise,
But listen to thee (walking in thy chamber)
Melting melodious words to lutes of amber.

ROBERT HERRICK

Maeve

You walk unaware
Of the slender gazelle
That moves as you move
And is one with the limbs
That you have.

You live unaware
Of the faint, the unearthly
Echo of hooves
That within your white streams
Of clear clay that I love

Are in flight as you turn,
As you stand, as you move,
As you sleep, for the slender
Gazelle never rests
In your ivory grove.

MERVYN PEAKE

25

The Discovery

I wandered to a crude coast
    Like a ghost;
Upon the hills I saw fires –
    Funeral pyres
Seemingly – and heard breaking
Waves like distant cannonades that set the land shaking.

And so I never once guessed
    A Love-nest,
Bowered and candle-lit, lay
    In my way,
Till I found a hid hollow,
Where I burst on her my heart could not but follow.

THOMAS HARDY

Ice (Vienna)
For Muriel

She came in from the snowing air
Where icicle-hung architecture
Strung white fleece round the Baroque square.
I saw her face freeze in her fur,
Then my lips ran to her with fire
From the chimney corner of the room,
Where I had waited in my chair.
I kissed their heat against her skin
And watched the red make the white bloom,
While, at my care, her smiling eyes
Shone with the brilliance of the ice
Outside, whose dazzling they brought in.
    That day, until this, I forgot.
How is it now I so remember
Who, when she came indoors, saw not
The passion of her white December?

STEPHEN SPENDER

Sonnet XXX from *Amoretti*

My love is like to ice, and I to fire;
How comes it then that this her cold so great
Is not dissolved through my so hot desire,
But harder grows the more I her entreat?
Or how comes it that my exceeding heat
Is not delayed by her heart frozen cold:
But that I burn much more in boiling sweat,
And feel my flames augmented manifold?
What more miraculous thing may be told
That fire which all things melts, should harden ice?
And ice which is congealed with senseless cold
Should kindle fire by wonderful device?
 Such is the power of love in gentle mind
 That it can alter all the course of kind.

EDMUND SPENSER

A Lover's Plea

Shall I come, sweet Love, to thee,
    When the evening beams are set?
Shall I not excluded be?
    Will you find no feignèd let?
Let me not, for pity, more
Tell the long hours at your door.

Who can tell what thief or foe
    In the covert of the night
For his prey will work my woe,
    Or through wicked foul despite?
So may I die unredressed,
Ere my long love be possessed.

But to let such dangers pass,
    Which a lover's thoughts disdain,
'Tis enough in such a place
    To attend love's joys in vain.
Do not mock me in thy bed,
While these cold nights freeze me dead.

THOMAS CAMPION

The Wedding Morning

The maidens came
    When I was in my mother's bower;
I had all that I would.
    The bailey beareth the bell away;
    The lily, the rose, the rose I lay.
The silver is white, red is the gold;
The robes they lay in fold.
    The bailey beareth the bell away;
    The lily, the rose, the rose I lay.
And through the glass window shines the sun.
How should I love, and I so young?
    The bailey beareth the bell away;
    The lily, the rose, the rose I lay.

ANON

Leda and the Swan

A sudden blow: the great wings beating still
Above the staggering girl, her thighs caressed
By the dark webs, her nape caught in his bill,
He holds her helpless breast upon his breast.

How can those terrified vague fingers push
The feathered glory from her loosening thighs?
And how can body, laid in that white rush,
But feel the strange heart beating where it lies?

A shudder in the loins engenders there
The broken wall, the burning roof and tower
And Agamemnon dead.
                Being so caught up,
So mastered by the brute blood of the air,
Did she put on his knowledge with his power
Before the indifferent beak could let her drop?

W. B. YEATS

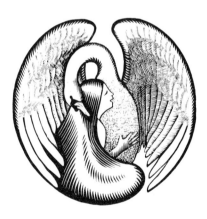

The Farmer's Bride

Three summers since I chose a maid,
Too young may be – but more's to do
At harvest-time than bide and woo.
    When us was wed she turned afraid
Of love and me and all things human;
Like the shut of a winter's day
Her smile went out, and 'twasn't a woman –
    More like a little frightened fay.
        One night, in the Fall, she runned away.

'Out 'mong the sheep, her be,' they said.
Should properly have been abed;
    But sure enough she wadn't there
    Lying awake with her wide brown stare.
Over seven-acre field and up-along across the down
    We chased her, flying like a hare
    Before our lanterns. To Church-Town
        All in a shiver and a scare
    We caught her, fetched her home at last
        And turned the key upon her, fast.

She does the work about the house
As well as most, but like a mouse:
    Happy enough to chat and play
    With birds and rabbits and such as they,
    So long as men-folk keep away.
'Not near, not near!' her eyes beseech
When one of us comes within reach.
    The women say that beasts in stall
    Look round like children at her call.
    I've hardly heard her speak at all.

Shy as a leveret, swift as he,
Straight and slight as a young larch tree,
Sweet as the first wild violets, she,
To her wild self. But what to me?

The short days shorten and the oaks are brown,
    The blue smoke rises to the low grey sky,
One leaf in the still air falls slowly down,
    A magpie's spotted feathers lie
On the black earth spread white with rime,
The berries redden up to Christmas-time.
    What's Christmas-time without there be
    Some other in the house than we!

    She sleeps up in the attic there
    Alone, poor maid. 'Tis but a stair
    Betwixt us. Oh! my God! the down,
    The soft young down of her, the brown,
The brown of her – her eyes, her hair, her hair!

CHARLOTTE MEW

Dread

Beside a chapel I'd a room looked down,
Where all the women from the farms and town,
On Holy-days, and Sundays used to pass
To marriages, and Christenings and to Mass.

Then I sat lonely watching score and score,
Till I turned jealous of the Lord next door . . .
Now by this window, where there's none can see,
The Lord God's jealous of yourself and me.

J. M. SYNGE

may i feel said he
(i'll squeal said she
just once said he)
it's fun said she

(may i touch said he
how much said she
a lot said he)
why not said she

(let's go said he
not too far said she
what's too far said he
where you are said she)

may i stay said he
(which way said she
like this said he
if you kiss said she

may i move said he
is it love said she)
if you're willing said he
(but you're killing said she

but it's life said he
but your wife said she
now said he)
ow said she

(tiptop said he
don't stop said she
oh no said he)
go slow said she

(cccome?said he
ummm said she)
you're divine! said he
(you are Mine said she)

   e. e. cummings

Meeting at Night

The grey sea and the long black land;
And the yellow half-moon large and low;
And the startled little waves that leap
In fiery ringlets from their sleep,
As I gain the cove with pushing prow,
And quench its speed i' the slushy sand.

Then a mile of warm sea-scented beach;
Three fields to cross till a farm appears;
A tap at the pane, the quick sharp scratch
And blue spurt of a lighted match,
And a voice less loud, through its joys and fears,
Than the two hearts beating each to each!

ROBERT BROWNING

Wild nights

Wild nights! Wild nights!
Were I with thee,
Wild nights should be
Our luxury!

Futile the winds
To a heart in port –
Done with the compass,
Done with the chart.

Rowing in Eden!
Ah! the sea!
Might I but moor
Tonight in thee!

EMILY DICKINSON

I'll Make My Love
a Breast of Glass

I'll make my love a breast of glass
And a heart of the porcelain white
The red blood seen through this clear window
Will stain it now dark now light.
I will make my love a head of gold
With hair of the black crow's feather
Her eyeballs of diamonds set therein
To crackle like thundery weather.

I'll make my love two arms of ice
Two hands of the rigid snow
I'll make my love two legs of flame
That will char the grass as they go.
I will make her a belly of the round moonlight
And the secret parts beneath
I will make of stars in a rainy night
Now hidden now gleaming like teeth.

To travel thereunder is my hope and my joy
To travel thereunder alone
An uncertain ride on a pitching road
Between black mire and sharp stone.
But what I will make, I will make and set up
In the corner of my love's crooked room
That she may regard it and learn from its shape
With what contrast of lust I consume.

I will make my love this image to love
And upon its hard brow I will write:
'This dream is my love yet you are my love
And who can tell which in the night?'
I will serve her in duty with flesh like an oak
And yet she will never know
How strong and how often I am serving the other
Stark naked in fire and in snow.

JOHN ARDEN

I Knew a Woman

I knew a woman, lovely in her bones,
When small birds sighed, she would sigh back at them;
Ah, when she moved, she moved more ways than one:
The shapes a bright container can contain!
Of her choice virtues only gods should speak,
Or English poets who grew up on Greek
(I'd have them sing in chorus, cheek to cheek).

How well her wishes went! She stroked my chin,
She taught me Turn, and Counter-turn, and Stand;
She taught me Touch, that undulant white skin;
I nibbled meekly from her proffered hand;
She was the sickle; I, poor I, the rake,
Coming behind her for her pretty sake
(But what prodigious mowing we did make).

Love likes a gander, and adores a goose:
Her full lips pursed, the errant note to seize;
She played it quick, she played it light and loose;
My eyes, they dazzled at her flowing knees;
Her several parts could keep a pure repose,
Or one hip quiver with a mobile nose
(She moved in circles, and those circles moved).

Let seed be grass, and grass turn into hay:
I'm martyr to a motion not my own;
What's freedom for? To know eternity.
I swear she cast a shadow white as stone.
But who would count eternity in days?
These old bones live to learn her wanton ways:
(I measure time by how a body sways).

THEODORE ROETHKE

Lust

How should I know? The enormous wheels of will
    Drove me cold-eyed on tired and sleepless feet.
Night was void arms and you a phantom still,
    And day your far light swaying down the street.
As never fool for love, I starved for you;
    My throat was dry and my eyes hot to see.
Your mouth so lying was most heaven to view,
    And your remembered smell most agony.

Love wakens love! I felt your hot wrist shiver,
    And suddenly the mad victory I planned
        Flashed real, in your burning bending head . . .
My conqueror's blood was cool as a deep river
    In shadow; and my heart beneath your hand
        Quieter than a dead man on a bed.

RUPERT BROOKE

A Last Confession

What lively lad most pleasured me
Of all that with me lay?
I answer that I gave my soul
And loved in misery,
But had great pleasure with a lad
That I loved bodily.

Flinging from his arms I laughed
To think his passion such
He fancied that I gave a soul
Did but our bodies touch,
And laughed upon his breast to think
Beast gave beast as much.

I gave what other women gave
That stepped out of their clothes,
But when this soul, its body off,
Naked to naked goes,
He it has found shall find therein
What none other knows.

And give his own and take his own
And rule in his own right;
And though it loved in misery
Close and cling so tight,
There's not a bird of day that dare
Extinguish that delight.

W. B. YEATS

Love's
Comfort

*

'Heart of the heartless world'

Sonnet 29

When, in disgrace with Fortune and men's eyes,
I all alone beweep my outcast state,
And trouble deaf heaven with my bootless cries,
And look upon myself and curse my fate,
Wishing me like to one more rich in hope,
Featured like him, like him with friends possessed,
Desiring this man's art, and that man's scope,
With what I most enjoy contented least;
Yet in these thoughts myself almost despising,
Haply I think on thee, and then my state,
Like to the lark at break of day arising
From sullen earth, sings hymns at heaven's gate;
    For thy sweet love remember'd such wealth brings,
    That then I scorn to change my state with kings.

WILLIAM SHAKESPEARE

She walks in beauty

She walks in beauty, like the night
    Of cloudless climes and starry skies;
And all that's best of dark and bright
    Meet in her aspect and her eyes:
Thus mellowed to that tender light
    Which heaven to gaudy day denies.

One shade the more, one ray the less,
    Had half impaired the nameless grace
Which waves in every raven tress,
    Or softly lightens o'er her face;
Where thoughts serenely sweet express
    How pure, how dear their dwelling-place.

And on that cheek, and o'er that brow,
    So soft, so calm, yet eloquent,
The smiles that win, the tints that glow,
    But tell of days in goodness spent,
A mind at peace with all below,
    A heart whose love is innocent.

LORD BYRON

The Silken Tent

She is as in a field a silken tent
At midday when a sunny summer breeze
Has dried the dew and all its ropes relent,
So that in guys it gently sways at ease,
And its supporting central cedar pole,
That is its pinnacle to heavenward
And signifies the sureness of the soul,
Seems to owe naught to any single cord,
But strictly held by none, is loosely bound
By countless silken ties of love and thought
To everything on earth the compass round,
And only by one's going slightly taut
In the capriciousness of summer air
Is of the slightest bondage made aware.

ROBERT FROST

To Helen

Helen, thy beauty is to me
    Like those Nicèan barks of yore
That gently, o'er a perfumed sea,
    The weary way-worn wanderer bore
    To his own native shore.

On desperate seas long wont to roam,
    Thy hyacinth hair, thy classic face,
Thy Naiad airs have brought me home
    To the glory that was Greece,
And the grandeur that was Rome.

Lo, in yon brilliant window-niche
    How statue-like I see thee stand,
    The agate lamp within thy hand,
Ah! Psyche, from the regions which
    Are holy land!

EDGAR ALLAN POE

48

O sweetheart, hear you

O sweetheart, hear you
    Your lover's tale;
A man shall have sorrow
    When friends him fail.

For he shall know then
    Friends be untrue
And a little ashes
    Their words come to.

But one unto him
    Will softly move
And softly woo him
    In ways of love.

His hand is under
    Her smooth round breast;
So he who has sorrow
    Shall have rest.

JAMES JOYCE

Ruth

She stood breast high amid the corn,
Clasped by the golden light of morn,
Like the sweetheart of the sun,
Who many a glowing kiss had won.

On her cheek an autumn flush,
Deeply ripened; – such a blush
In the midst of brown was born,
Like red poppies grown with corn.

Round her eyes her tresses fell,
Which were blackest none could tell,
But long lashes veiled a light,
That had else been all too bright.

And her hat, with shady brim,
Made her tressy forehead dim; –
Thus she stood amid the stooks,
Praising God with sweetest looks: –

Sure, I said, heaven did not mean,
Where I reap thou shouldst but glean,
Lay thy sheaf adown and come,
Share my harvest and my home.

THOMAS HOOD

Homecomings

I

Fetch me the sandmartin
skimming and veering
breast to breast with himself
in the clouds in the river.

II

At the worn mouth of the hole
flight after flight after flight
the swoop of his wings
gloved and kissed home.

III

A glottal stillness. An eardrum.
Far in, featherbrains tucked in silence,
a silence of water
lipping the bank.

IV

Mould my shoulders inward to you.
Occlude me.
Be damp clay pouting.
Let me listen under your eaves.

SEAMUS HEANEY

51

from *The Princess*

Now sleeps the crimson petal, now the white;
Nor waves the cypress in the palace walk;
Nor winks the gold fin in the porphyry font:
The fire-fly wakens: waken thou with me.

Now droops the milkwhite peacock like a ghost,
And like a ghost she glimmers on to me.

Now lies the Earth all Danaë to the stars,
And all thy heart lies open unto me.

Now slides the silent meteor on, and leaves
A shining furrow, as thy thoughts in me.

Now folds the lily all her sweetness up,
And slips into the bosom of the lake:
So fold thyself, my dearest, thou, and slip
Into my bosom and be lost in me.

ALFRED, LORD TENNYSON

Lovers

You were glad to-night: and now you've gone away.
Flushed in the dark, you put your dreams to bed;
But as you fall asleep I hear you say
Those tired sweet drowsy words we left unsaid.

Sleep well: for I can follow you, to bless
And lull your distant beauty where you roam;
And with wild songs of hoarded loveliness
Recall you to these arms that were your home.

SIEGFRIED SASSOON

My shy hand

My shy hand shades a hermitage apart, –
    O large enough for thee, and thy brief hours.
Life there is sweeter held than in God's heart,
    Stiller than in the heavens of hollow flowers.

The wine is gladder there than in gold bowls.
    And Time shall not drain thence, nor trouble spill.
Sources between my fingers feed all souls,
    Where thou mayest cool thy lips, and draw thy fill.

Five cushions hath my hand, for reveries;
    And one deep pillow for thy brow's fatigues;
Languor of June all winterlong, and ease
    For ever from the vain untravelled leagues.

Thither your years may gather in from storm,
And Love, that sleepeth there, will keep thee warm.

WILFRED OWEN

When I heard at the
close of the day

When I heard at the close of the day how my name
    had been receiv'd with plaudits in the capitol, still
    it was not a happy night for me that follow'd,
And else when I carous'd, or when my plans were
    accomplish'd, still I was not happy,
But the day when I rose at dawn from the bed of
    perfect health, refresh'd, singing, inhaling the
    ripe breath of autumn,
When I saw the full moon in the west grow pale and
    disappear in the morning light,
When I wander'd alone over the beach, and
    undressing bathed, laughing with the cool waters,
    and saw the sun rise,
And when I thought how my dear friend my lover
    was on his way coming, O then I was happy,
O then each breath tasted sweeter, and all that day
    my food nourish'd me more, and the beautiful
    day pass'd well,
And the next came with equal joy, and with the next
    at evening came my friend,
And that night while all was still I heard the waters
    roll slowly continually up the shores,
I heard the hissing rustle of the liquid and sands as
    directed to me whispering to congratulate me,
For the one I love most lay sleeping by me under the
    same cover in the cool night,
In the stillness in the autumn moonbeams his face
    was inclined toward me,
And his arm lay lightly around my breast – and that
    night I was happy.

WALT WHITMAN

She Tells Her Love While Half Asleep

She tells her love while half asleep
   In the dark hours,
      With half-words whispered low:
As Earth stirs in her winter sleep
   And puts out grass and flowers
      Despite the snow,
      Despite the falling snow.

ROBERT GRAVES

Winter Love

Let us have winter loving that the heart
May be in peace and ready to partake
Of the slow pleasure spring would wish to hurry
Or that in summer harshly would awake,
And let us fall apart, O gladly weary,
The white skin shaken like a white snowflake.

ELIZABETH JENNINGS

The Confirmation

Yes, yours, my love, is the right human face.
I in my mind had waited for this long,
Seeing the false and searching for the true,
Then found you as a traveller finds a place
Of welcome suddenly amid the wrong
Valleys and rocks and twisting roads. But you,
What shall I call you? A fountain in a waste,
A well of water in a country dry,
Or anything that's honest and good, an eye
That makes the whole world bright. Your open heart,
Simple with giving, gives the primal deed,
The first good world, the blossom, the blowing seed,
The hearth, the steadfast land, the wandering sea,
Not beautiful or rare in every part,
But like yourself, as they were meant to be.

EDWIN MUIR

Sonnet 130

My mistress' eyes are nothing like the sun;
Coral is far more red than her lips' red;
If snow be white, why then her breasts are dun;
If hairs be wires, black wires grow on her head.
I have seen roses damasked, red and white,
But no such roses see I in her cheeks,
And in some perfumes is there more delight
Than in the breath that from my mistress reeks.
I love to hear her speak, yet well I know
That music hath a far more pleasing sound.
I grant I never saw a goddess go;
My mistress when she walks treads on the ground.
    And yet, by heaven, I think my love as rare
    As any she belied with false compare.

WILLIAM SHAKESPEARE

And You, Helen

And you, Helen, what should I give you?
So many things I would give you
Had I an infinite great store
Offered me and I stood before
To choose. I would give you youth,
All kinds of loveliness and truth.
A clear eye as good as mine,
Lands, waters, flowers, wine,
As many children as your heart
Might wish for, a far better art
Than mine can be, all you have lost
Upon the travelling waters tossed,
Or given to me. If I could choose
Freely in that great treasure-house
Anything from any shelf,
I would give you back yourself,
And power to discriminate
What you want and want it not too late,
Many fair days free from care
And heart to enjoy both foul and fair,
And myself, too, if I could find
Where it lay hidden and it proved kind.

EDWARD THOMAS

from *Sonnets from the Portuguese*

If thou must love me, let it be for naught
   Except for love's sake only. Do not say,
    'I love her for her smile – her look – her way
Of speaking gently, – for a trick of thought
That falls in well with mine, and certes brought
   A sense of pleasant ease on such a day' –
   For these things in themselves, Beloved, may
Be changed, or change for thee – and love, so wrought,
May be unwrought so. Neither love me for
   Thine own dear pity's wiping my cheeks dry:
A creature might forget to weep, who bore
   Thy comfort long, and lose thy love thereby!
But love me for love's sake, that evermore
   Thou mayst love on, through love's eternity.

ELIZABETH BARRETT BROWNING

Goodbye

So we must say Goodbye, my darling,
And go, as lovers go, for ever;
Tonight remains, to pack and fix on labels
And make an end of lying down together.

I put a final shilling in the gas,
And watch you slip your dress below your knees
And lie so still I hear your rustling comb
Modulate the autumn in the trees.

And all the countless things I shall remember
Lay mummy-cloths of silence round my head;
I fill the carafe with a drink of water;
You say 'We paid a guinea for this bed,'

And then, 'We'll leave some gas, a little warmth
For the next resident, and these dry flowers,'
And turn your face away, afraid to speak
The big word, that Eternity is ours.

Your kisses close my eyes and yet you stare
As though God struck a child with nameless fears;
Perhaps the water glitters and discloses
Time's chalice and its limpid useless tears.

Everything we renounce except our selves;
Selfishness is the last of all to go;
Our sighs are exhalations of the earth,
Our footprints leave a track across the snow.

We made the universe to be our home,
Our nostrils took the wind to be our breath,
Our hearts are massive towers of delight,
We stride across the seven seas of death.

Yet when all's done you'll keep the emerald
I placed upon your finger in the street;
And I will keep the patches that you sewed
On my old battledress tonight, my sweet.

ALUN LEWIS

Postscript: For Gweno

If I should go away,
Beloved, do not say
'He has forgotten me'.
For you abide,
A singing rib within my dreaming side;
You always stay.
And in the mad tormented valley
Where blood and hunger rally
And Death the wild beast is uncaught, untamed,
Our soul withstands the terror
And has its quiet honour
Among the glittering stars your voices named.

ALUN LEWIS

Huesca

Heart of the heartless world,
Dear heart, the thought of you
Is the pain at my side,
The shadow that chills my view.

The wind rises in the evening,
Reminds that autumn is near.
I am afraid to lose you,
I am afraid of my fear.

On the last mile to Huesca,
The last fence for our pride,
Think so kindly, dear, that I
Sense you at my side.

And if bad luck should lay my strength
Into the shallow grave,
Remember all the good you can;
Don't forget my love.

JOHN CORNFORD

Love and Time

*

'Between the tiger's paws'

Feste's Song from *Twelfth Night*

O mistress mine, where are you roaming?
O! stay and hear; your true love's coming,
    That can sing both high and low.
Trip no further, pretty sweeting;
Journeys end in lovers meeting,
    Every wise man's son doth know.

What is love? 'Tis not hereafter;
Present mirth hath present laughter;
    What's to come is still unsure.
In delay there lies no plenty;
Then come kiss me, sweet and twenty;
    Youth's a stuff will not endure.

WILLIAM SHAKESPEARE

To His Coy Mistress

Had we but world enough, and time,
This coyness, Lady, were no crime.
We would sit down, and think which way
To walk, and pass our long love's day.
Thou by the Indian Ganges' side
Shouldst rubies find: I by the tide
Of Humber would complain. I would
Love you ten years before the flood:
And you should, if you please, refuse
Till the conversion of the Jews.
My vegetable love should grow
Vaster than empires, and more slow.
An hundred years should go to praise
Thine eyes, and on thy forehead gaze.
Two hundred to adore each breast:
But thirty thousand to the rest.
An age at least to every part,
And the last age should show your heart:
For, Lady, you deserve this state;
Nor would I love at lower rate.
    But at my back I always hear
Time's wingèd chariot hurrying near:
And yonder all before us lie
Deserts of vast eternity.
Thy beauty shall no more be found;
Nor, in thy marble vault, shall sound
My echoing song: then worms shall try
That long preserved virginity:
And your quaint honour turn to dust;
And into ashes all my lust.
The grave's a fine and private place,
But none, I think, do there embrace.
    Now, therefore, while the youthful hue
Sits on thy skin like morning dew,
And while thy willing soul transpires
At every pore with instant fires,

Now let us sport us while we may;
And now, like amorous birds of prey,
Rather at once our time devour,
Than languish in his slow-chapped power.
Let us roll all our strength, and all
Our sweetness, up into one ball:
And tear our pleasures with rough strife,
Thorough the iron gates of life.
Thus, though we cannot make our sun
Stand still, yet we will make him run.

ANDREW MARVELL

Piazza Piece

– I am a gentleman in a dustcoat trying
To make you hear. Your ears are soft and small
And listen to an old man not at all,
They want the young men's whispering and sighing.
But see the roses on your trellis dying
And hear the spectral singing of the moon;
For I must have my lovely lady soon,
I am a gentleman in a dustcoat trying.

– I am a lady young in beauty waiting
Until my truelove comes, and then we kiss.
But what grey man among the vines is this
Whose words are dry and faint as in a dream?
Back from my trellis, Sir, before I scream!
I am a lady young in beauty waiting.

JOHN CROWE RANSOM

72

Go, Lovely Rose

Go, lovely Rose –
   Tell her that wastes her time and me,
   That now she knows,
When I resemble her to thee,
How sweet and fair she seems to be.

   Tell her that's young,
And shuns to have her graces spied,
   That hadst thou sprung
In deserts where no men abide,
Thou must have uncommended died.

   Small is the worth
Of beauty from the light retired:
   Bid her come forth,
Suffer herself to be desired,
And not blush so to be admired.

   Then die – that she
The common fate of all things rare
   May read in thee;
How small a part of time they share
That are so wondrous sweet and fair!

EDMUND WALLER

73

Song

Out upon it, I have loved
　　Three whole days together;
And am like to love three more,
　　If it hold fair weather.

Time shall moult away his wings
　　Ere he shall discover
In the whole wide world again
　　Such a constant lover.

But a pox upon't, no praise
　　There is due at all to me:
Love with me had made no stays,
　　Had it any been but she.

Had it any been but she
　　And that very very face,
There had been at least ere this
　　A dozen dozen in her place.

SIR JOHN SUCKLING

Love and Life

All my past life is mine no more;
    The flying hours are gone,
Like transitory dreams given o'er
Whose images are kept in store
    By memory alone.

Whatever is to come is not:
    How can it then be mine?
The present moment's all my lot,
And that, as fast as it is got,
    Phyllis, is wholly thine.

Then talk not of inconstancy,
    False hearts, and broken vows;
If I, by miracle, can be
This livelong minute true to thee,
    'Tis all that heaven allows.

JOHN WILMOT, EARL OF ROCHESTER

'Not Marble Nor the Gilded Monuments'

The praisers of women in their proud and beautiful poems,
Naming the grave and the hair and the eyes,
Boasted those they loved should be forever remembered:
These were lies.

The words sound but the face in the Istrian sun is forgotten.
The poet speaks but to her dead ears no more.
The sleek throat is gone – and the breast that was troubled to
    listen:
Shadow from door.

Therefore I will not praise your knees nor your fine walking
Telling you men shall remember your name as long
As lips move or breath is spent or the iron of English
Rings from a tongue.

I shall say you were young, and your arms straight, and your
    mouth scarlet:
I shall say you will die and none will remember you:
Your arms change, and none remember the swish of your
    garments,
Nor the click of your shoe.

Not with my hand's strength, not with difficult labor
Springing the obstinate words to the bones of your breast
And the stubborn line to your young stride and the breath to
    your breathing
And the beat to your haste
Shall I prevail on the hearts of unborn men to remember.

(What is a dead girl but a shadowy ghost
Or a dead man's voice but a distant and vain affirmation
Like dream words most)

Therefore I will not speak of the undying glory of women.
I will say you were young and straight and your skin fair
And you stood in the door and the sun was a shadow of leaves
    on your shoulders
And a leaf on your hair –
    I will not speak of the famous beauty of dead women:
    I will say the shape of a leaf lay once on your hair.
    Till the world ends and the eyes are out and the mouths
        broken,
    Look! It is there!

ARCHIBALD MACLEISH

The Hill

Breathless, we flung us on the windy hill,
　　Laughed in the sun, and kissed the lovely grass.
　　You said, 'Through glory and ecstasy we pass;
Wind, sun, and earth remain, the birds sing still,
When we are old, are old. . .' 'And when we die
　　All's over that is ours; and life burns on
Through other lovers, other lips,' said I,
　　'Heart of my heart, our heaven is now, is won!'
'We are Earth's best, that learnt her lesson here.
　　Life is our cry. We have kept the faith!' we said;
　　'We shall go down with unreluctant tread
Rose-crowned into the darkness! . . .' Proud we were,
　　And laughed, that had such brave true things to say.
　　And then you suddenly cried, and turned away.

RUPERT BROOKE

from *Modern Love*

We saw the swallows gathering in the sky,
And in the osier-isle we heard them noise.
We had not to look back on summer joys,
Or forward to a summer of bright dye:
But in the largeness of the evening earth
Our spirits grew as we went side by side.
The hour became her husband and my bride.
Love, that had robbed us so, thus blessed our dearth!
The pilgrims of the year waxed very loud
In multitudinous chatterings, as the flood
Full brown came from the West, and like pale blood
Expanded to the upper crimson cloud.
Love, that had robbed us of immortal things,
This little moment mercifully gave,
Where I have seen across the twilight wave
The swan sail with her young beneath her wings.

GEORGE MEREDITH

A Song

Absent from thee, I languish still;
    Then ask me not, when I return?
The straying fool 'twill plainly kill
    To wish all day, all night to mourn.

Dear! from thine arms then let me fly,
    That my fantastic mind may prove
The torments it deserves to try
    That tears my fixed heart from my love.

When, wearied with a world of woe,
    To thy safe bosom I retire
Where love and peace and truth does flow,
    May I contented there expire,

Lest, once more wandering from that heaven,
    I fall on some base heart unblest,
Faithless to thee, false, unforgiven,
    And lose my everlasting rest.

JOHN WILMOT, EARL OF ROCHESTER

Warm are the still and lucky miles

Warm are the still and lucky miles,
White shores of longing stretch away,
A light of recognition fills
    The whole great day, and bright
The tiny world of lovers' arms.

Silence invades the breathing wood
Where drowsy limbs a treasure keep,
Now greenly falls the learned shade
    Across the sleeping brows
And stirs their secret to a smile.

Restored! Returned! The lost are borne
On seas of shipwreck home at last:
See! In a fire of praising burns
    The dry dumb past, and we
Our life-day long shall part no more.

W. H. AUDEN

Lullaby

Lay your sleeping head, my love,
Human on my faithless arm;
Time and fevers burn away
Individual beauty from
Thoughtful children, and the grave
Proves the child ephemeral:
But in my arms till break of day
Let the living creature lie,
Mortal, guilty, but to me
The entirely beautiful.

Soul and body have no bounds:
To lovers as they lie upon
Her tolerant enchanted slope
In their ordinary swoon,
Grave the vision Venus sends
Of supernatural sympathy,
Universal love and hope;
While an abstract insight wakes
Among the glaciers and the rocks
The hermit's carnal ecstasy.

Certainty, fidelity
On the stroke of midnight pass
Like vibrations of a bell
And fashionable madmen raise
Their pedantic boring cry:
Every farthing of the cost,
All the dreaded cards foretell,
Shall be paid, but from this night
Not a whisper, not a thought,
Not a kiss nor look be lost.

Beauty, midnight, vision dies:
Let the winds of dawn that blow
Softly round your dreaming head
Such a day of welcome show
Eye and knocking heart may bless,
Find our mortal world enough;
Noons of dryness find you fed
By the involuntary powers,
Nights of insult let you pass
Watched by every human love.

W. H. AUDEN

In Love For Long

I've been in love for long
With what I cannot tell
And will contrive a song
For the intangible
That has no mould or shape,
From which there's no escape.

It is not even a name,
Yet is all constancy;
Tried or untried, the same,
It cannot part from me;
A breath, yet as still
As the established hill.

It is not any thing,
And yet all being is;
Being, being, being,
Its burden and its bliss.
How can I ever prove
What it is I love?

This happy happy love
Is sieged with crying sorrows,
Crushed beneath and above
Between todays and morrows;
A little paradise
Held in the world's vice.

And there it is content
And careless as a child,
And in imprisonment
Flourishes sweet and wild;
In wrong, beyond wrong,
All the world's day long.

This love a moment known
For what I do not know
And in a moment gone
Is like the happy doe
That keeps its perfect laws
Between the tiger's paws
And vindicates its cause.

EDWIN MUIR

from *Trilogy for X*

I

When clerks and navvies fondle
  Beside canals their wenches,
In rapture or in coma
  The haunches that they handle,
And the orange moon sits idle
  Above the orchard slanted –
Upon such easy evenings
  We take our loves for granted.

But when, as now, the creaking
  Trees on the hills of London
Like bison charge their neighbours
  In wind that keeps us waking
And in the draught the scalloped
  Lampshade swings a shadow,
We think of love bound over –
  The mortgage on the meadow.

And one lies lonely, haunted
  By limbs he half remembers,
And one, in wedlock, wonders
  Where is the girl he wanted;
And some sit smoking, flicking
  The ash away and feeling
For love gone up like vapour
  Between the floor and ceiling.

But now when winds are curling
  The trees do you come closer,
Close as an eyelid fasten
  My body in darkness, darling;
Switch the light off and let me
  Gather you up and gather
The power of trains advancing
  Further, advancing further.

86

II

And love hung still as crystal over the bed
    And filled the corners of the enormous room;
The boom of dawn that left her sleeping, showing
    The flowers mirrored in the mahogany table.

O my love, if only I were able
    To protract this hour of quiet after passion,
Not ration happiness but keep this door for ever
    Closed on the world, its own world closed within it.

But dawn's waves trouble with the bubbling minute,
    The names of books come clear upon their shelves,
The reason delves for duty and you will wake
    With a start and go on living on your own.

The first train passes and the windows groan,
    Voices will hector and your voice become
A drum in tune with theirs, which all last night
    Like sap that fingered through a hungry tree
Asserted our one night's identity.

LOUIS MACNEICE

87

At the Dark Hour

Our love was conceived in silence and must live silently.
This only our sorrow, and this until the end.
Listen, did we not lie all of one evening,
Your heart under my hand

And no word spoken, no, not even the sighing
Of pain made comfortable, not the heart's beat
Nor sound of urgency, but a fire dying
And the cold sheet?

The sailor goes home singing; the lamplit lovers
Make private movements in a public place.
Boys whistle under windows, and are answered;
But we must hold our peace.

Day, too, broke silently. Before the blackbird,
Before the trouble of traffic and the mist unrolled,
I shall remember at the dark hour turning to you
For comfort in the cold.

PAUL DEHN

The Room Above the Square

The light in the window seemed perpetual
Where you stayed in the high room for me;
It flowered above the trees through leaves
Like my certainty.

The light is fallen and you are hidden
In sunbright peninsulas of the sword:
Torn like leaves through Europe is the peace
Which through me flowed.

Now I climb alone to the dark room
Which hangs above the square
Where among stones and roots the other
Peaceful lovers are.

STEPHEN SPENDER

Two in the Campagna

I wonder do you feel to-day
　　As I have felt since, hand in hand,
We sat down on the grass, to stray
　　In spirit better through the land,
This morn of Rome and May?

For me, I touched a thought, I know,
　　Has tantalized me many times,
(Like turns of thread the spiders throw
　　Mocking across our path) for rhymes
To catch at and let go.

Help me to hold it! First it left
　　The yellowing fennel, run to seed
There, branching from the brickwork's cleft,
　　Some old tomb's ruin: yonder weed
Took up the floating weft,

Where one small orange cup amassed
　　Five beetles, – blind and green they grope
Among the honey-meal: and last,
　　Everywhere on the grassy slope
I traced it. Hold it fast!

The champaign with its endless fleece
　　Of feathery grasses everywhere!
Silence and passion, joy and peace,
　　An everlasting wash of air –
Rome's ghost since her decease.

Such life here, through such lengths of hours,
　　Such miracles performed in play,
Such primal naked forms of flowers,
　　Such letting nature have her way
While heaven looks from its towers!

How say you? Let us, O my dove,
 Let us be unashamed of soul,
As earth lies bare to heaven above!
 How is it under our control
To love or not to love?

I would that you were all to me,
 You that are just so much, no more.
Nor yours nor mine, nor slave nor free!
 Where does the fault lie? What the core
O' the wound, since wound must be?

I would I could adopt your will,
 See with your eyes, and set my heart
Beating by yours, and drink my fill
 At your soul's springs, – your part my part
In life, for good and ill.

No. I yearn upward, touch you close,
 Then stand away. I kiss your cheek,
Catch your soul's warmth, – I pluck the rose
 And love it more than tongue can speak –
Then the good minute goes.

Already how am I so far
 Out of that minute? Must I go
Still like the thistle-ball, no bar,
 Onward, whenever light winds blow,
Fixed by no friendly star?

Just when I seemed about to learn!
 Where is the thread now? Off again!
The old trick! Only I discern –
 Infinite passion, and the pain
Of finite hearts that yearn.

ROBERT BROWNING

To Mary

The twentieth year is well-nigh past,
Since first our sky was overcast;
Ah would that this might be the last!
                 My Mary!

Thy spirits have a fainter flow,
I see thee daily weaker grow –
'Twas my distress that brought thee low,
                 My Mary!

Thy needles, once a shining store,
For my sake restless heretofore,
Now rust disus'd, and shine no more,
                 My Mary!

For though thou gladly wouldst fulfil
The same kind office for me still,
Thy sight now seconds not thy will,
                 My Mary!

But well thou play'dst the housewife's part,
And all thy threads with magic art
Have wound themselves about this heart,
                 My Mary!

Thy indistinct expressions seem
Like language utter'd in a dream;
Yet me they charm, whate'er the theme,
                 My Mary!

Thy silver locks, once auburn bright,
Are still more lovely in my sight
Than golden beams of orient light,
                 My Mary!

For could I view nor them nor thee,
What sight worth seeing could I see?
The sun would rise in vain for me,
                    My Mary!

Partakers of thy sad decline,
Thy hands their little force resign;
Yet, gently prest, press gently mine,
                    My Mary!

And then I feel that still I hold
A richer store ten thousandfold
Than misers fancy in their gold,
                    My Mary!

Such feebleness of limbs thou prov'st,
That now at every step thou mov'st
Upheld by two; yet still thou lov'st,
                    My Mary!

And still to love, though prest with ill,
In wintry age to feel no chill,
With me is to be lovely still,
                    My Mary!

But ah! by constant heed I know.
How oft the sadness that I show
Transforms thy smiles to looks of woe,
                    My Mary!

And should my future lot be cast
With much resemblance of the past,
Thy worn-out heart will break at last,
                    My Mary!

WILLIAM COWPER

from *Sonnets from the Portuguese*

When our two souls stand up erect and strong,
    Face to face, silent, drawing nigh and nigher,
    Until the lengthening wings break into fire
At either curvèd point, – what bitter wrong
Can the earth do to us, that we should not long
    Be here contented? Think. In mounting higher,
    The angels would press on us and aspire
To drop some golden orb of perfect song
Into our deep, dear silence. Let us stay
    Rather on earth, Beloved, – where the unfit,
Contrarious moods of men recoil away
    And isolate pure spirits, and permit
A place to stand and love in for a day,
    With darkness and the death-hour rounding it.

ELIZABETH BARRETT BROWNING

Verses Made the Night
Before He Died

So well I love thee as without thee I
Love nothing; if I might choose, I'd rather die
Than be one day debarred thy company.

Since beasts and plants do grow and live and move,
Beasts are those men that such a life approve:
He only lives that deadly is in love.

The corn, that in the ground is sown, first dies,
And of one seed do many ears arise;
Love, this world's corn, by dying multiplies.

The seeds of love first by thy eyes were thrown
Into a ground untilled, a heart unknown
To bear such fruit, till by thy hands 'twas sown.

Look as your looking-glass by chance may fall,
Divide, and break in many pieces small,
And yet shows forth the selfsame face in all,

Proportions, features, graces, just the same,
And in the smallest piece as well the name
Of fairest one deserves as in the richest frame;

So all my thoughts are pieces but of you,
Which put together makes a glass so true
As I therein no other's face but yours can view.

MICHAEL DRAYTON

95

Love's Anguish

*

'Can you endure such grief . . . ?'

Death and Love

Though I am young, and cannot tell
  Either what Death or Love is well,
Yet I have heard they both bear darts,
  And both do aim at human hearts;
And then again I have been told
  Love wounds with heat, as Death with cold;
So that I fear they do but bring
  Extremes to touch, and mean one thing.

As in a ruin, we it call
  One thing to be blown up or fall;
Or to our end like way may have,
  By a flash of lightning or a wave:
So Love's inflamèd shaft or brand
  May kill as soon as Death's cold hand;
Except Love's fires the virtue have
  To fright the frost out of the grave.

BEN JONSON

99

A Leave-Taking

Let us go hence, my songs; she will not hear.
Let us go hence together without fear;
Keep silence now, for singing-time is over,
And over all old things and all things dear.
She loves not you nor me as we all love her.
Yea, though we sang as angels in her ear,
   She would not hear.

Let us rise up and part; she will not know.
Let us go seaward as the great winds go,
Full of blown sand and foam; what help is here?
There is no help, for all these things are so,
And all the world is bitter as a tear.
And how these things are, though ye strove to show,
   She would not know.

Let us go home and hence; she will not weep.
We gave love many dreams and days to keep,
Flowers without scent, and fruits that would not grow,
Saying, 'If thou wilt, thrust in thy sickle and reap.'
All is reaped now; no grass is left to mow;
And we that sowed, though all we fell on sleep,
   She would not weep.

Let us go hence and rest; she will not love.
She shall not hear us if we sing hereof,
Nor see love's ways, how sore they are and steep.
Come hence, let be, lie still; it is enough.
Love is a barren sea, bitter and deep;
And though she saw all heaven in flower above,
   She would not love.

Let us give up, go down; she will not care.
Though all the stars made gold of all the air,
And the sea moving saw before it move
One moon-flower making all the foam-flowers fair;
Though all those waves went over us, and drove
Deep down the stifling lips and drowning hair,
        She would not care.

Let us go hence, go hence; she will not see.
Sing all once more together; surely she,
She too, remembering days and words that were,
Will turn a little toward us, sighing; but we,
We are hence, we are gone, as though we had not been there.
Nay, and though all men seeing had pity on me,
        She would not see.

ALGERNON CHARLES SWINBURNE

101

The Gourmet's Love-Song

How strange is Love; I am not one
    Who Cupid's power belittles,
For Cupid 'tis who makes me shun
    My customary victuals.
Oh, EFFIE, since that painful scene
    That left me broken-hearted,
My appetite, erstwhile so keen,
    Has utterly departed.

My form, my friends observe with pain,
    Is growing daily thinner.
Love only occupies the brain
    That once could think of dinner.
Around me myriad waiters flit,
    With meat and drink to ply men;
Alone, disconsolate, I sit,
    And feed on thoughts of Hymen.

The kindly waiters hear my groan,
    They strive to charm with curry;
They tempt me with a devilled bone –
    I beg them not to worry.
Soup, whitebait, entrées, fricassees,
    They bring me uninvited.
I need them not, for what are these
    To one whose life is blighted?

They show me dishes rich and rare,
    But ah! my pulse no joy stirs.
For savouries I've ceased to care,
    I hate the thought of oysters.
They bring me roast, they bring me boiled,
    But all in vain they woo me;
The waiters softly mutter, 'Foiled!'
    The chef, poor man, looks gloomy.

So, EFFIE, turn that shell-like ear,
    Nor to my sighing close it,
You cannot doubt that I'm sincere –
    This ballad surely shows it.
No longer spurn the suit I press,
    Respect my agitation,
Do change your mind, and answer, 'Yes',
    And save me from starvation.

P. G. WODEHOUSE

A Silent Love

The lowest trees have tops, the ant her gall,
The fly her spleen, the little spark his heat;
The slender hairs cast shadows, though but small,
And bees have stings, although they be not great;
    Seas have their source, and so have shallow springs;
    And love is love, in beggars and in kings.

Where waters smoothest run, there deepest are the fords,
The dial stirs, yet none perceives it move;
The firmest faith is found in fewest words,
The turtles do not sing, and yet they love;
    True hearts have ears and eyes, no tongues to speak;
    They hear and see, and sigh, and then they break.

SIR EDWARD DYER

Symptoms of Love

Love is a universal migraine,
A bright stain on the vision
Blotting out reason.

Symptoms of true love
Are leanness, jealousy,
Laggard dawns;

Are omens and nightmares –
Listening for a knock,
Waiting for a sign:

For a touch of her fingers
In a darkened room,
For a searching look.

Take courage, lover!
Can you endure such grief
At any hand but hers?

ROBERT GRAVES

This living hand

This living hand, now warm and capable
Of earnest grasping, would, if it were cold
And in the icy silence of the tomb,
So haunt thy days and chill thy dreaming nights
That thou wouldst wish thine own heart dry of blood
So in my veins red life might stream again,
And thou be conscience-calmed – see here it is –
I hold it towards you.

JOHN KEATS

No Second Troy

Why should I blame her that she filled my days
With misery, or that she would of late
Have taught to ignorant men most violent ways,
Or hurled the little streets upon the great,
Had they but courage equal to desire?
What could have made her peaceful with a mind
That nobleness made simple as a fire,
With beauty like a tightened bow, a kind
That is not natural in an age like this,
Being high and solitary and most stern?
Why, what could she have done, being what she is?
Was there another Troy for her to burn?

W. B. YEATS

O my thoughts' sweet food

O my thoughts' sweet food, my my only owner,
O my heaven's foretaste by thy heavenly pleasure,
O the fair nymph born to do women honour,
                    Lady my treasure:

Where be now those joys that I lately tasted?
Where be now those eyes, ever inly piercers?
Where be now those words never idly wasted,
                    Wounds to rehearsers?

Where is, ah, that face, that a sun defaces?
Where be those welcomes, by no worth deserved?
Where be those movings, the delights, the graces?
                    How be we swerved?

O hideous absence, by thee am I thralled:
O my vain word gone, ruin of my glory!
O due allegiance, by thee am I called
                    Still to be sorry.

But no more words, though such a word be spoken,
Nor no more wording, with a word to spill me:
Peace, due allegiance; duty must be broken
                    If duty kill me.

Then come, O come; then do I come, receive me,
Slay me not, for stay; do not hide thy blisses,
But between those arms; never else do leave me;
                    Give me my kisses.

O my thoughts' sweet food, my my only owner,
O my heaven's foretaste by thy heavenly pleasure,
O the fair nymph born to do women honour,
                    Lady my treasure.

SIR PHILIP SIDNEY

I cry your mercy, pity, love

I cry your mercy, pity, love – aye love!
   Merciful love that tantalizes not
One-thoughted, never-wandering, guileless love,
   Unmasked, and being seen – without a blot!
Oh, let me have thee whole, – all, all, be mine!
   That shape, that fairness, that sweet minor zest
Of love, your kiss – those hands, those eyes divine,
   That warm, white, lucent, million-pleasured breast;
Yourself – your soul – in pity give me all,
   Withhold no atom's atom or I die;
Or living on, perhaps, your wretched thrall,
   Forget, in the mist of idle misery,
Life's purposes – the palate of my mind
Losing its gust, and my ambition blind!

JOHN KEATS

Sonnet 62 from *Astrophil and Stella*

Late tired with woe, even ready for to pine
With rage of love, I called my love unkind;
She in whose eyes love, though unfelt, doth shine,
Sweet said that I true love in her should find.
    I joyed, but straight thus watered was my wine,
That love she did, but loved a love not blind,
Which would not let me, whom she loved, decline
From nobler course, fit for my birth and mind:
    And therefore, by her love's authority,
    Willed me these tempests of vain love to fly,
And anchor fast myself on virtue's shore.
    Alas, if this the only metal be
    Of love, new-coined to help my beggary,
Dear, love me not, that you may love me more.

SIR PHILIP SIDNEY

Sonnet 147

My love is as a fever, longing still
For that which longer nurseth the disease,
Feeding on that which doth preserve the ill,
The uncertain sickly appetite to please.
My reason, the physician to my love,
Angry that his prescriptions are not kept,
Hath left me, and I desperate now approve
Desire is death, which physic did except.
Past cure I am, now Reason is past care,
And frantic-mad with evermore unrest;
My thoughts and my discourse as madmen's are,
At random from the truth vainly expressed.
    For I have sworn thee fair, and thought thee bright,
    Who art as black as hell, as dark as night.

WILLIAM SHAKESPEARE

A Forge, and a Scythe

One minute I had the windows open
and the sun was out. Warm breezes
blew through the room.
(I remarked on this in a letter.)
Then, while I watched, it grew dark.
The water began whitecapping.
All the sport-fishing boats turned
and headed in, a little fleet.
Those wind-chimes on the porch
blew down. The tops of our trees shook.
The stove pipe squeaked and rattled
around in its moorings.
I said, 'A forge, and a scythe.'
I talk to myself like this.
Saying the names of things –
capstan, hawser, loam, leaf, furnace.
Your face, your mouth, your shoulder
inconceivable to me now!
Where did they go? It's like
I dreamed them. The stones we brought
home from the beach lie face up
on the windowsill, cooling.
Come home. Do you hear?
My lungs are thick with the smoke
of your absence.

RAYMOND CARVER

Images

I

Like a gondola of green scented fruits
Drifting along the dark canals of Venice,
You, O exquisite one,
Have entered my desolate city.

II

The blue smoke leaps
Like swirling clouds of birds vanishing.
So my love leaps towards you
Vanishes and is renewed.

III

A rose-yellow moon in a pale sky
When the sunset is faint vermilion
On the mist among the tree-boughs
Are you to me.

IV

As a young beech-tree on the edge of a forest
Stands still in the evening,
Then shudders through all its leaves in the light air
And seems to fear the stars –
So are you still and so tremble.

V

The red deer are high on the mountain,
They are beyond the last pine-trees.
And my desires have run with them.

VI

The flower which the wind has shaken
Is soon filled again with rain:
So does my heart fill slowly with tears
Until you return.

RICHARD ALDINGTON

Envoi

Take of me what is not my own,
my love, my beauty, and my poem –
the pain is mine, and mine alone.

See how against the weight in the bone
the hawk hangs perfect in mid-air –
the blood pays dear to raise it there,
the moment, not the bird, divine.

And see the peaceful trees extend
their myriad leaves in leisured dance –
they bear the weight of sky and cloud
upon the fountain of their veins.

In rose with petals soft as air
I bind for you the tides and fire –
the death that lives within the flower,
oh gladly, love, for you I bear!

KATHLEEN RAINE

Renouncement

I must not think of thee; and, tired yet strong,
I shun the thought that lurks in all delight –
    The thought of thee – and in the blue heaven's height,
And in the sweetest passage of a song.
Oh, just beyond the fairest thoughts that throng
    This breast, the thought of thee waits hidden yet bright;
But it must never, never come in sight;
I must stop short of thee the whole day long.
But when sleep comes to close each difficult day,
   When night gives pause to the long watch I keep,
And all my bonds I needs must loose apart,
Must doff my will as raiment laid away, –
    With the first dream that comes with the first sleep
I run, I run, I am gathered to thy heart.

ALICE MEYNELL

The Broken Heart

He is stark mad, who ever says
    That he hath been in love an hour,
Yet not that love so soon decays,
    But that it can ten in less space devour;
Who will believe me, if I swear
That I have had the plague a year?
      Who would not laugh at me, if I should say,
      I saw a flask of powder burn a day?

Ah, what a trifle is a heart,
    If once into Love's hands it come!
All other griefs allow a part
    To other griefs, and ask themselves but some,
They come to us, but us Love draws,
He swallows us, and never chaws:
      By him, as by chain-shot, whole ranks do die,
      He is the tyrant pike, our hearts the fry.

If 'twere not so, what did become
    Of my heart, when I first saw thee?
I brought a heart into the room,
    But from the room, I carried none with me;
If it had gone to thee, I know
Mine would have taught thy heart to show
      More pity unto me: but Love, alas,
      At one first blow did shiver it as glass.

Yet nothing can to nothing fall,
    Nor any place be empty quite,
Therefore I think my breast hath all
    Those pieces still, though they be not unite;
And now as broken glasses show
A hundred lesser faces, so
      My rags of heart can like, wish, and adore,
      But after one such love, can love no more.

JOHN DONNE

Non sum qualis eram bonae sub regno Cynarae

Last night, ah, yesternight, betwixt her lips and mine
There fell thy shadow, Cynara! thy breath was shed
Upon my soul between the kisses and the wine;
And I was desolate and sick of an old passion,
   Yea, I was desolate and bowed my head:
I have been faithful to thee, Cynara! in my fashion.

All night upon mine heart I felt her warm heart beat,
Night-long within mine arms in love and sleep she lay;
Surely the kisses of her bought red mouth were sweet;
But I was desolate and sick of an old passion,
   When I awoke and found the dawn was grey:
I have been faithful to thee, Cynara! in my fashion.

I have forgot much, Cynara! gone with the wind,
Flung roses, roses riotously with the throng,
Dancing, to put thy pale, lost lilies out of mind;
But I was desolate and sick of an old passion,
   Yea, all the time, because the dance was long:
I have been faithful to thee, Cynara! in my fashion.

I cried for madder music and for stronger wine,
But when the feast is finished and the lamps expire,
Then falls thy shadow, Cynara! the night is thine;
And I am desolate and sick of an old passion,
   Yea, hungry for the lips of my desire:
I have been faithful to thee, Cynara! in my fashion.

ERNEST DOWSON

A Broken Appointment

You did not come,
And marching Time drew on, and wore me numb.
Yet less for loss of your dear presence there
Than that I thus found lacking in your make
That high compassion which can overbear
Reluctance for pure lovingkindness' sake
Grieved I, when, as the hope-hour stroked its sum
You did not come.

You love not me,
And love alone can lend you loyalty;
– I know and knew it. But, unto the store
Of human deeds divine in all but name,
Was it not worth a little hour or more
To add yet this: Once you, a woman, came
To soothe a time-torn man; even though it be
You love not me?

THOMAS HARDY

I hear an army

I hear an army charging upon the land,
    And the thunder of horses plunging, foam about their knees:
Arrogant, in black armour, behind them stand,
    Disdaining the reins, with fluttering whips, the charioteers.

They cry unto the night their battle-name:
    I moan in sleep when I hear afar their whirling laughter.
They cleave the gloom of dreams, a blinding flame,
    Clanging, clanging upon the heart as upon an anvil.

They come shaking in triumph their long, green hair:
    They come out of the sea and run shouting by the shore.
My heart, have you no wisdom thus to despair?
    My love, my love, my love, why have you left me alone?

JAMES JOYCE

Annihilation

While the blue noon above us arches,
And the poplar sheds disconsolate leaves,
Tell me again why love bewitches,
And what love gives.

Is it the trembling finger that traces
The eyebrow's curve, the curve of the cheek?
The mouth that quivers, while the hand caresses,
But cannot speak?

No, not these, not in these is hidden
The secret, more than in other things:
Not only the touch of a hand can gladden
Till the blood sings.

It is the leaf that falls between us,
The bell that murmurs, the shadows that move,
The autumnal sunlight that fades upon us:
These things are love.

It is the 'No, let us sit here longer,'
The 'Wait till tomorrow,' the 'Once I knew – '
These trifles, said as you touch my finger,
And the clock strikes two.

The world is intricate, and we are nothing.
It is the complex world of grass,
The twig on the path, a look of loathing,
Feelings that pass –

These are the secret! And I could hate you,
When, as I lean for another kiss,
I see in your eyes that I do not meet you,
And that love is this.

Rock meeting rock can know love better
Than eyes that stare or lips that touch.
All that we know in love is bitter,
And it is not much.

CONRAD AIKEN

Sonnet 57

Being your slave, what should I do but tend
Upon the hours and times of your desire?
I have no precious time at all to spend,
Nor services to do till you require.
Nor dare I chide the world-without-end hour
Whilst I, my sovereign, watch the clock for you,
Nor think the bitterness of absence sour
When you have bid your servant once adieu.
Nor dare I question with my jealous thought
Where you may be, or your affairs suppose,
But, like a sad slave, stay and think of naught
Save where you are how happy you make those.
　So true a fool is love that in your will,
　Though you do anything, he thinks no ill.

WILLIAM SHAKESPEARE

Iambicum Trimetrum

Unhappy Verse, the witness of my unhappy state,
   Make thyself fluttering wings of thy fast flying
   Thought, and fly forth unto my Love, wheresoever she be:
Whether lying restless in heavy bed, or else
   Sitting so cheerless at the cheerful board, or else
   Playing alone careless on her heavenly virginals.
If in bed, tell her that my eyes can take no rest;
   If at board, tell her that my mouth can eat no meat;
   If at her virginals, tell her I can hear no mirth.
Asked why? say, Waking love suffereth no sleep;
   Say that raging love doth appal the weak stomach;
   Say that lamenting love marreth the musical.
Tell her that her pleasures were wont to lull me asleep;
   Tell her that her beauty was wont to feed mine eyes;
   Tell her that her sweet tongue was wont to make me mirth.
Now do I nightly waste, wanting my kindly rest;
   Now do I daily starve, wanting my lively food;
   Now do I always die, wanting thy timely mirth.
And if I waste, who will bewail my heavy chance?
   And if I starve, who will record my cursed end?
   And if I die, who will say, *this was Immerito?*

EDMUND SPENSER

To Earthward

Love at the lips was touch
As sweet as I could bear;
And once that seemed too much;
I lived on air.

That crossed me from sweet things,
The flow of – was it musk
From hidden grapevine springs
Down hill at dusk?

I had the swirl and ache
From the sprays of honeysuckle
That when they're gathered shake
Dew on the knuckle.

I craved strong sweets, but those
Seemed strong when I was young;
The petal of the rose
It was that stung.

Now no joy but lacks salt
That is not dashed with pain
And weariness and fault;
I crave the stain

Of tears the aftermark
Of almost too much love,
The sweet of bitter bark
And burning clove.

When stiff and sore and scarred
I take away my hand
From leaning on it hard
In grass and sand,

The hurt is not enough:
I long for weight and strength
To feel the earth as rough
To all my length.

ROBERT FROST

Beautiful Despair

I look at the moon,
And the frail silver of the climbing stars;
I look, dear, at you,
And I cast my verses away.

EDWARD STORER

Love's
Failure

*

'I am a star that is dead'

To the Tune of
the Coventry Carol

The nearly right
And yet not quite
In love is wholly evil
And every heart
That loves in part
Is mortgaged to the devil.

I loved or thought
I loved in sort
Was this to love akin
To take the best
And leave the rest
And let the devil in?

O lovers true
And others too
Whose best is only better
Take my advice
Shun compromise
Forget him and forget her.

STEVIE SMITH

The Sick Rose

O rose, thou art sick!
The invisible worm
That flies in the night,
In the howling storm,

Has found out thy bed
Of crimson joy,
And his dark secret love
Does thy life destroy.

WILLIAM BLAKE

The Window Sill

Presage and caveat not only seem
To come in dream,
But do so come in dream.

When the cock crew and phantoms floated by,
This dreamer I
Out of the house went I,

Down long unsteady streets to a mad square;
And who was there,
Or whom did I know there?

Julia, leaning on her window sill.
'I love you still,'
She said, 'O love me still!'

I answered: 'Julia, do you love me best?'
'What of this breast,'
She mourned, 'this flowery breast?'

Then a wild sobbing spread from door to door,
And every floor
Cried shame on every floor,

As she unlaced her bosom to disclose
Each breast a rose,
A white and cankered rose.

ROBERT GRAVES

La Figlia che Piange

Stand on the highest pavement of the stair –
Lean on a garden urn –
Weave, weave the sunlight in your hair –
Clasp your flowers to you with a pained surprise –
Fling them to the ground and turn
With a fugitive resentment in your eyes:
But weave, weave the sunlight in your hair.

So I would have had him leave,
So I would have had her stand and grieve,
So he would have left
As the soul leaves the body torn and bruised,
As the mind deserts the body it has used.
I should find
Some way incomparably light and deft,
Some way we both should understand,
Simple and faithless as a smile and shake of the hand.

She turned away, but with the autumn weather
Compelled my imagination many days,
Many days and many hours:
Her hair over her arms and her arms full of flowers.
And I wonder how they should have been together!
I should have lost a gesture and a pose.
Sometimes these cogitations still amaze
The troubled midnight and the noon's repose.

T. S. ELIOT

Severed Selves
from *The House of Life*

Two separate divided silences,
    Which, brought together, would find loving voice;
    Two glances which together would rejoice
In love, now lost like stars beyond dark trees;
Two hands apart whose touch alone gives ease;
    Two bosoms which, heart-shrined with mutual flame,
    Would, meeting in one clasp, be made the same;
Two souls, the shores wave mocked of sundering seas: –

Such are we now. Ah! may our hope forecast
    Indeed one hour again, when on this stream
    Of darkened love once more the light shall gleam? –
An hour how slow to come, how quickly past, –
Which blooms and fades, and only leaves at last,
    Faint as shed flowers, the attenuated dream.

DANTE GABRIEL ROSSETTI

Like the touch of rain

Like the touch of rain she was
On a man's flesh and hair and eyes
When the joy of walking thus
Has taken him by surprise:

With the love of the storm he burns,
He sings, he laughs, well I know how,
But forgets when he returns
As I shall not forget her 'Go now.'

Those two words shut a door
Between me and the blessed rain
That was never shut before
And will not open again.

EDWARD THOMAS

The Terrible Door

Too long outside your door I have shivered.
You open it? I will not stay.
I'm haunted by your ashen beauty.
Take back your hand. I have gone away.

Don't talk, but move to that near corner.
I loathe the long cold shadow here.
We will stand a moment in the lamplight,
Until I watch you hard and near.

Happy release! Good-bye for ever!
Here at the corner we say good-bye.
But if you want me, if you do need me,
Who waits, at the terrible door, but I?

HAROLD MONRO

When we two parted

When we two parted
    In silence and tears,
Half broken-hearted
    To sever for years,
Pale grew thy cheek and cold,
    Colder thy kiss;
Truly that hour foretold
    Sorrow to this.

The dew of the morning
    Sunk chill on my brow –
It felt like the warning
    Of what I feel now.
Thy vows are all broken,
    And light is thy fame;
I hear thy name spoken,
    And share in its shame.

They name thee before me,
    A knell to mine ear;
A shudder comes o'er me –
    Why wert thou so dear?
They know not I knew thee,
    Who knew thee too well: –
Long, long shall I rue thee,
    Too deeply to tell.

In secret we met –
    In silence I grieve,
That thy heart could forget,
    Thy spirit deceive.
If I should meet thee
    After long years,
How should I greet thee?
    With silence and tears.

LORD BYRON

Remembrance

They flee from me, that sometime did me seek
   With naked foot, stalking in my chamber.
I have seen them gentle, tame, and meek,
    That now are wild, and do not remember
    That sometime they put themselves in danger
      To take bread at my hand; and now they range
      Busily seeking with a continual change.

Thanked be fortune it hath been otherwise
   Twenty times better; but once, in special,
In thin array, after a pleasant guise,
    When her loose gown from her shoulders did fall,
    And she me caught in her arms long and small,
      Therewith all sweetly did me kiss
      And softly said, 'Dear heart, how like you this?'

It was no dream; I lay broad waking:
   But all is turned, thorough my gentleness,
Into a strange fashion of forsaking;
    And I have leave to go of her goodness,
    And she also to use newfangleness.
      But since that I so kindly am served,
      I would fain know what she hath deserved.

SIR THOMAS WYATT

Never Seek to Tell thy Love

Never seek to tell thy love
Love that never told can be;
For the gentle wind does move
Silently, invisibly.

I told my love, I told my love,
I told her all my heart,
Trembling, cold, in ghastly fears –
Ah, she doth depart.

Soon as she was gone from me
A traveller came by
Silently, invisibly –
O, was no deny.

WILLIAM BLAKE

Because I liked you better

Because I liked you better
 Than suits a man to say,
It irked you, and I promised
 To throw the thought away.

To put the world between us
 We parted, stiff and dry;
'Good-bye', said you, 'forget me.'
 'I will, no fear', said I.

If here, where clover whitens
 The dead man's knoll, you pass,
And no tall flower to meet you
 Starts in the trefoiled grass,

Halt by the headstone naming
 The heart no longer stirred,
And say the lad that loved you
 Was one that kept his word.

A. E. HOUSMAN

Scarborough Fair

Where are you going? To Scarborough Fair.
Parsley, sage, rosemary, thyme,
Remember me to a bonny lass there,
For once she was a true lover of mine.

Tell her to make me a cambric shirt,
Parsley, sage, rosemary, thyme,
Without any needle or thread worked in't,
And she shall be a true lover of mine.

Tell her to wash it in yonder well,
Parsley, sage, rosemary, thyme,
Where water ne'er sprung nor a drop of rain fell,
And she shall be a true lover of mine.

Tell her to plough me an acre of land,
Parsley, sage, rosemary, thyme,
Between the sea and the salt sea strand,
And she shall be a true lover of mine.

Tell her to plough it with one ram's horn,
Parsley, sage, rosemary, thyme,
And sow it all over with one peppercorn,
And she shall be a true lover of mine.

Tell her to reap it with a sickle of leather,
Parsley, sage, rosemary, thyme,
And tie it all up with a tom tit's feather,
And she shall be a true lover of mine.

Tell her to gather it all in a sack,
Parsley, sage, rosemary, thyme,
And carry it home on a butterfly's back,
And then she shall be a true lover of mine.

ANON

I am a lamp, a lamp that is out

I am a lamp, a lamp that is out;
    I am a shallow stream;
In it are neither pearls or trout,
    Nor one of the things that you dream.

Why do you smile and deny, my lover?
    I will not be denied.
I am a book, a book with a cover,
    And nothing at all inside.

Here is the truth, and you must grapple,
    Grapple with what I have said.
I am a dumpling without any apple,
    I am a star that is dead.

FRANCES CORNFORD

By the Lake

Across the thick and the pastel snow
Two people go. . . . 'And do you remember
When last we wandered this shore?' . . . 'Ah no!
For it is cold-hearted December.'
'Dead, the leaves that like asses' ears hung on the trees
When last we wandered and squandered joy here;
Now Midas your husband will listen for these
Whispers – these tears for joy's bier.'
And as they walk, they seem tall pagodas;
And all the ropes let down from the cloud
Ring the hard cold bell-buds upon the trees – codas
Of overtones, ecstasies, grown for love's shroud.

EDITH SITWELL

Song

O lady, when the tipped cup of the moon blessed you
You became soft fire with a cloud's grace;
The difficult stars swam for eyes in your face;
You stood, and your shadow was my place:
You turned, your shadow turned to ice
    O my lady.

O lady, when the sea caressed you
You were a marble of foam, but dumb.
When will the stone open its tomb?
When will the waves give over their foam?
You will not die, nor come home,
    O my lady.

O lady, when the wind kissed you
You made him music for you were a shaped shell.
I follow the waters and the wind still
Since my heart heard it and all to pieces fell
Which your lovers stole, meaning ill,
    O my lady.

O lady, consider when I shall have lost you
The moon's full hands, scattering waste,
The sea's hands, dark from the world's breast,
The world's decay where the wind's hands have passed,
And my head, worn out with love, at rest
In my hands, and my hands full of dust,
    O my lady.

TED HUGHES

To Marguerite

Yes! in the sea of life enisled,
With echoing straits between us thrown,
Dotting the shoreless watery wild,
We mortal millions live *alone*.
The islands feel the enclasping flow,
And then their endless bounds they know.

But when the moon their hollows lights,
And they are swept by balms of spring,
And in their glens, on starry nights,
The nightingales divinely sing;
And lovely notes, from shore to shore,
Across the sounds and channels pour –

Oh! then a longing like despair
Is to their farthest caverns sent;
For surely once, they feel, we were
Parts of a single continent!
Now round us spreads the watery plain –
Oh might our marges meet again!

Who ordered, that their longing's fire
Should be, as soon as kindled, cooled?
Who renders vain their deep desire? –
A God, a God their severance ruled!
And bade betwixt their shores to be
The unplumbed, salt, estranging sea.

MATTHEW ARNOLD

Sea Love

Tide be runnin' the great world over:
    'Twas only last June month I mind that we
Was thinkin' the toss and the call in the breast of the lover
    So everlastin' as the sea.

Heer's the same little fishes that sputter and swim,
    Wi' the moon's old glim on the grey, wet sand;
An' him no more to me nor me to him
    Than the wind goin' over my hand.

CHARLOTTE MEW

She Walked Unaware

Oh, she walked unaware of her own increasing beauty
That was holding men's thoughts from market or plough,
As she passed by intent on her womanly duties
And she passed without leisure to be wayward or proud;
Or if she had pride then it was not in her thinking
But thoughtless in her body like a flower of good breeding.
The first time I saw her spreading coloured linen
Beyond the green willow she gave me gentle greeting
With no more intention than the leaning willow tree.

Though she smiled without intention yet from that day forward
Her beauty filled like water the four corners of my being,
And she rested in my heart like a hare in the form
That is shaped to herself. And I that would be singing
Or whistling at all times went silently then,
Till I drew her aside among straight stems of beeches
When the blackbird was sleeping and she promised that never
The fields would be ripe but I'd gather all sweetness,
A red moon of August would rise on our wedding.

October is spreading bright flame along stripped willows,
Low fires of the dogwood burn down to grey water, –
God pity me now and all desolate sinners
Demented with beauty! I have blackened my thought
In drouths of bad longing, and all brightness goes shrouded
Since he came with his rapture of wild words that mirrored
Her beauty and made her ungentle and proud.
Tonight she will spread her brown hair on his pillow,
But I shall be hearing the harsh cries of wild fowl.

PATRICK MACDONOGH

Will Not Come Back

Dark swallows will doubtless come back killing
the injudicious nightflies with a clack of the beak;
but these that stopped full flight to see your beauty
and my good fortune . . . as if they knew our names –
they'll not come back. The thick lemony honeysuckle,
climbing from the earthroot to your window,
will open more beautiful blossoms to the evening;
but these . . . like dewdrops, trembling, shining, falling,
the tears of day – they'll not come back . . .
Some other love will sound his fireword for you
and wake your heart, perhaps, from its cool sleep;
but silent, absorbed, and on his knees,
as men adore God at the altar, as I love you –
don't blind yourself, you'll not be loved like that.

ROBERT LOWELL

147

'My True Love Hath My Heart
and I Have His'

None ever was in love with me but grief.
    She wooed me from the day that I was born;
She stole my playthings first, the jealous thief,
    And left me there forlorn.

The birds that in my garden would have sung,
    She scared away with her unending moan;
She slew my lovers too when I was young,
    And left me there alone.

Grief, I have cursed thee often – now at last
    To hate thy name I am no longer free;
Caught in thy bony arms and prisoned fast,
    I love no love but thee.

MARY COLERIDGE

The Lost Mistress

All's over, then: does truth sound bitter
    As one at first believes?
Hark, 'tis the sparrows' good-night twitter
    About your cottage eaves!

And the leaf-buds on the vine are woolly,
    I noticed that, today;
One day more bursts them open fully
    – You know the red turns grey.

Tomorrow we meet the same then, dearest?
    May I take your hand in mine?
Mere friends are we, – well, friends the merest
    Keep much that I resign:

For each glance of the eye so bright and black,
    Though I keep with heart's endeavour, –
Your voice, when you wish the snowdrops back,
    Though it stay in my soul for ever! –

Yet I will but say what mere friends say,
    Or only a thought stronger;
I will hold your hand but as long as all may,
    Or so very little longer!

ROBERT BROWNING

Oh, when I was in love with you

Oh, when I was in love with you,
    Then I was clean and brave,
And miles around the wonder grew
    How well did I behave.

And now the fancy passes by,
    And nothing will remain,
And miles around they'll say that I
    Am quite myself again.

A. E. HOUSMAN

Song from *Marriage à la Mode*

Why should a foolish marriage vow,
    Which long ago was made,
Oblige us to each other now,
    When passion is decayed?
We loved, and we loved, as long as we could,
    Till our love was loved out in us both;
But our marriage is dead, when the pleasure is fled:
    'Twas pleasure first made it an oath.

If I have pleasures for a friend,
    And farther love in store,
What wrong has he whose joys did end,
    And who could give no more?
'Tis a madness that he should be jealous of me,
    Or that I should bar him of another:
For all we can gain is to give ourselves pain,
    When neither can hinder the other.

JOHN DRYDEN

Intimates

Don't you care for my love? she said bitterly.

I handed her the mirror, and said:
Please address these questions to the proper person!
Please make all requests to head-quarters!
In all matters of emotional importance
please approach the supreme authority direct! –
So I handed her the mirror.

And she would have broken it over my head,
but she caught sight of her own reflection
and that held her spellbound for two seconds
while I fled.

D. H. LAWRENCE

The Custom of the World

O, we loved long and happily, God knows!
The ocean danced, the green leaves tossed, the air
Was filled with petals, and pale Venus rose
When we began to kiss. Kisses brought care,
And closeness caused the taking off of clothes.
O, we loved long and happily, God knows!

'The watchdogs are asleep, the doormen doze . . .'
We huddled in the corners of the stair,
And then we climbed it. What had we to lose?
What would we gain? The best way to compare
And quickest, was by taking off our clothes.
O, we loved long and happily, God knows!

Between us two a silent treason grows,
Our pleasures have been changed into despair.
Wild is the wind, from a cold country blows,
In which these tender blossoms disappear.
And did this come of taking off our clothes?
O, we loved long and happily, God knows!

Mistress, my song is drawing to a close.
Put on your rumpled skirt and comb your hair,
And when we meet again let us suppose
We never loved or ever naked were.
For though this nakedness was good, God knows,
The custom of the world is wearing clothes.

LOUIS SIMPSON

O Waly, Waly

The water is wide, I cannot get o'er
And neither have I wings to fly.
Give me a boat that will carry two,
And both shall row, my love and I.

O, down in the meadows the other day,
A-gathering flowers both fine and gay,
A-gathering flowers both red and blue,
I little thought what love can do.

I leaned my back up against some oak,
Thinking that he was a trusty tree;
But first he bended and then he broke;
And so did my false love to me.

A ship there is, and she sails the sea,
She's loaded deep as deep can be,
But not so deep as the love I'm in:
I know not if I sink or swim.

O, love is handsome and love is fine,
And love's a jewel while it is new,
But when it is old, it groweth cold,
And fades away like morning dew.

ANON

Love's Memory

*

'Remember me when I am gone away'

Sudden Light

I have been here before,
    But when or how I cannot tell:
I know the grass beyond the door,
    The sweet keen smell,
The sighing sound, the lights around the shore.

You have been mine before, –
    How long ago I may not know:
But just when at that swallow's soar
    Your neck turned so,
Some veil did fall, – I knew it all of yore.

Has this been thus before?
    And shall not thus time's eddying flight
Still with our lives our love restore
    In death's despite,
And day and night yield one delight once more?

DANTE GABRIEL ROSSETTI

O western wind, when wilt thou blow
    That the small rain down can rain?
Christ! that my love were in my arms
    And I in my bed again.

ANON

The half-moon westers low, my love,
    And the wind brings up the rain;
And wide apart lie we, my love,
    And seas between the twain.

I know not if it rains, my love,
    In the land where you do lie;
And oh, so sound you sleep, my love,
    You know no more than I.

A. E. HOUSMAN

Glanmore Sonnets: X

I dreamt we slept in a moss in Donegal
On turf banks under blankets, with our faces
Exposed all night in a wetting drizzle,
Pallid as the dripping sapling birches.
Lorenzo and Jessica in a cold climate.
Diarmuid and Grainne waiting to be found.
Darkly asperged and censed, we were laid out
Like breathing effigies on a raised ground.
And in that dream I dreamt – how like you this? –
Our first night years ago in that hotel
When you came with your deliberate kiss
To raise us towards the lovely and painful
Covenants of flesh; our separateness;
The respite in our dewy dreaming faces.

SEAMUS HEANEY

Farewell to Juliet

I see you, Juliet, still, with your straw hat
Loaded with vines, and with your dear pale face,
On which those thirty years so lightly sat,
And the white outline of your muslin dress.
You wore a little *fichu* trimmed with lace
And crossed in front, as was the fashion then,
Bound at your waist with a broad band or sash,
All white and fresh and virginally plain.
There was a sound of shouting far away
Down in the valley, as they called to us,
And you, with hands clasped seeming still to pray
Patience of fate, stood listening to me thus
With heaving bosom. There a rose lay curled.
It was the reddest rose in all the world.

WILFRID BLUNT

As birds are fitted to the boughs

As birds are fitted to the boughs
That blossom on the tree
And whisper when the south wind blows –
So was my love to me.

And still she blossoms in my mind
And whispers softly, though
The clouds are fitted to the wind,
The wind is to the snow.

LOUIS SIMPSON

At Castle Boterel

As I drive to the junction of lane and highway,
  And the drizzle bedrenches the waggonette,
I look behind at the fading byway,
  And see on its slope, now glistening wet,
    Distinctly yet

Myself and a girlish form benighted
  In dry March weather. We climb the road
Beside a chaise. We had just alighted
  To ease the sturdy pony's load
    When he sighed and slowed.

What we did as we climbed, and what we talked of
  Matters not much, nor to what it led, –
Something that life will not be balked of
  Without rude reason till hope is dead,
    And feeling fled.

It filled but a minute. But was there ever
  A time of such quality, since or before,
In that hill's story? To one mind never,
  Though it has been climbed, foot-swift, foot-sore,
    By thousands more.

Primaeval rocks form the road's steep border,
  And much have they faced there, first and last,
Of the transitory in Earth's long order;
  But what they record in colour and cast
    Is – that we two passed.

And to me, though Time's unflinching rigour,
  In mindless rote, has ruled from sight
The substance now, one phantom figure
  Remains on the slope, as when that night
    Saw us alight.

I look and see it there, shrinking, shrinking,
     I look back at it amid the rain
For the very last time; for my sand is sinking,
     And I shall traverse old love's domain
          Never again.

THOMAS HARDY

Walsingham

'As you came from the holy land
    Of Walsingham,
Met you not with my true love
    By the way as you came?'

'How shall I know your true love,
    That have met many one
As I went to the holy land,
    That have come, that have gone?'

'She is neither white nor brown,
    But as the heavens fair,
There is none hath a form so divine
    In the earth or the air.'

'Such an one did I meet, good Sir,
    Such an angelic face,
Who like a queen, like a nymph did appear
    By her gait, by her grace.'

'She hath left me here all alone,
    All alone as unknown,
Who sometimes did me lead with herself,
    And me loved as her own.'

'What's the cause that she leaves you alone
    And a new way doth take,
Who loved you once as her own
    And her joy did you make?'

'I have loved her all my youth,
    But now old as you see,
Love likes not the falling fruit
    From the withered tree.

'Know that Love is a careless child,
    And forgets promise past;
He is blind, he is deaf when he list
    And in faith never fast.

'His desire is a dureless content
    And a trustless joy;
He is won with a world of despair
    And is lost with a toy.

'Of womenkind such indeed is the love
    Or the word love abused,
Under which many childish desires
    And conceits are excused.

'But true Love is a durable fire
    In the mind ever burning;
Never sick, never old, never dead,
    From itself never turning.'

SIR WALTER RALEGH

165

Raspberries

Once, as a child, I ate raspberries. And forgot.
And then, years later,
A raspberry flowered on my palate, and the past
Burst in unfolding layers within me.
It tasted of grass and honey.
You were there, watching and smiling.
Our love unfolded in the taste of raspberries.

More years have passed; and you are far, and ill;
And I, unable to reach you, eating raspberries.
Their dark damp red, their cool and fragile fur
On the always edge of decay, on the edge of bitter,
Bring a hush of taste to the mouth

Tasting of earth and of crushed leaves,
Tasting of summer's insecurity,
Tasting of crimson, dark with the smell of honey,
Tasting of childhood and of remembered childhood,
And now, now first, the darker taste of dread.

Sap and imprisoned sunlight and crushed grass
Lie on my tongue like a shadow,
Burst like impending news on my aching palate

Tasting not only of death (I could bear that)
But of death and of you together,
The folded layers of love and the sudden future,
Tasting of earth and the thought of you as earth

As I go on eating, waiting for the news.

LAURENCE LERNER

Song

A widow bird sat mourning for her love
    Upon a wintry bough;
The frozen wind crept on above,
    The freezing stream below.

There was no leaf upon the forest bare,
    No flower upon the ground,
And little motion in the air
    Except the mill-wheel's sound.

PERCY BYSSHE SHELLEY

Lucy

She dwelt among the untrodden ways
    Beside the springs of Dove,
A Maid whom there were none to praise
    And very few to love:

A violet by a mossy stone
    Half hidden from the eye!
Fair as a star, when only one
    Is shining in the sky.

She lived unknown, and few could know
    When Lucy ceased to be;
But she is in her grave, and oh,
    The difference to me!

WILLIAM WORDSWORTH

Surprised by joy

Surprised by joy – impatient as the wind
    I turned to share the transport – Oh! with whom
    But thee, deep buried in the silent tomb,
That spot which no vicissitude can find?
Love, faithful love, recalled thee to my mind –
    But how could I forget thee? Through what power,
    Even for the least division of an hour,
Have I been so beguiled as to be blind
To my most grievous loss! – That thought's return
    Was the worst pang that sorrow ever bore,
Save one, one only, when I stood forlorn,
    Knowing my heart's best treasure was no more;
That neither present time, nor years unborn
    Could to my sight that heavenly face restore.

WILLIAM WORDSWORTH

Annabel Lee

It was many and many a year ago,
    In a kingdom by the sea,
That a maiden there lived whom you may know
    By the name of Annabel Lee;
And this maiden she lived with no other thought
    Than to love and be loved by me.

I was a child and she was a child,
    In this kingdom by the sea;
But we loved with a love that was more than love –
    I and my Annabel Lee;
With a love that the winged seraphs of heaven
    Coveted her and me.

And this was the reason that, long ago
    In this kingdom by the sea,
A wind blew out of a cloud, chilling
    My beautiful Annabel Lee;
So that her highborn kinsman came
    And bore her away from me,
To shut her up in a sepulchre
    In this kingdom by the sea.

The angels, not half so happy in heaven,
    Went envying her and me –
Yes! – that was the reason (as all men know,
    In this kingdom by the sea)
That the wind came out of the cloud by night,
    Chilling and killing my Annabel Lee.

But our love it was stronger by far than the love
    Of those who were older than we,
    Of many far wiser than we;
And neither the angels in heaven above
    Nor the demons down under the sea
Can ever dissever my soul from the soul
    Of the beautiful Annabel Lee.

For the moon never beams without bringing me dreams
    Of the beautiful Annabel Lee;
And the stars never rise but I feel the bright eyes
    Of the beautiful Annabel Lee;
And so, all the night-tide, I lie down by the side
Of my darling – my darling – my life and my bride,
    In the sepulchre by the sea,
    In her tomb by the sounding sea.

EDGAR ALLAN POE

Requiescat

Tread lightly, she is near
    Under the snow,
Speak gently, she can hear
    The daisies grow.

All her bright golden hair
    Tarnished with rust,
She that was young and fair
    Fallen to dust.

Lily-like, white as snow,
    She hardly knew
She was a woman, so
    Sweetly she grew.

Coffin-board, heavy stone,
    Lie on her breast,
I vex my heart alone,
    She is at rest.

Peace, Peace, she cannot hear
    Lyre or sonnet,
All my life's buried here,
    Heap earth upon it.

OSCAR WILDE

An Epitaph Upon Husband and Wife, Which Died and Were Buried Together

To these whom death again did wed,
This grave's their second marriage bed;
For though the hand of fate could force
'Twixt soul and body a divorce,
It could not sunder man and wife
Because they both liv'd but one life.
Peace, good reader, do not weep;
Peace, the lovers are asleep.
They, sweet turtles, folded lie
In the last knot that love could tie.
And though they lie as they were dead,
Their pillows stone, their sheets of lead,
(Pillow hard, and sheets not warm)
Love made the bed; they'll take no harm.
Let them sleep, let them sleep on
Till this stormy night be gone,
Till th' eternal morrow dawn:
Till the curtains will be drawn,
And they awake into a light
Whose day shall never die in night.

RICHARD CRASHAW

His Late Wife's Wedding-Ring

The ring so worn, as you behold,
So thin, so pale, is yet of gold:
The passion such it was to prove;
Worn with life's cares, love yet was love.

GEORGE CRABBE

On His Dead Wife

Methought I saw my late espousèd saint
    Brought to me like Alcestis from the grave,
    Whom Jove's great son to her glad husband gave,
    Rescued from death by force, though pale and faint.
Mine, as whom washed from spot of childbed taint
    Purification in the old Law did save,
    And such as yet once more I trust to have
    Full sight of her in heaven without restraint,
Came vested all in white, pure as her mind.
    Her face was veiled, yet to my fancied sight
    Love, sweetness, goodness, in her person shined
So clear as in no face with more delight.
    But O as to embrace me she inclined,
    I waked, she fled, and day brought back my night.

JOHN MILTON

An Arundel Tomb

Side by side, their faces blurred,
The earl and countess lie in stone,
Their proper habits vaguely shown
As jointed armour, stiffened pleat,
And that faint hint of the absurd –
The little dogs under their feet.

Such plainness of the pre-baroque
Hardly involves the eye, until
It meets his left-hand gauntlet, still
Clasped empty in the other; and
One sees, with a sharp tender shock,
His hand withdrawn, holding her hand.

They would not think to lie so long.
Such faithfulness in effigy
Was just a detail friends would see:
A sculptor's sweet commissioned grace
Thrown off in helping to prolong
The Latin names around the base.

They would not guess how early in
Their supine stationary voyage
The air would change to soundless damage,
Turn the old tenantry away;
How soon succeeding eyes begin
To look, not read. Rigidly they

Persisted, linked, through lengths and breadths
Of time. Snow fell, undated. Light
Each summer thronged the glass. A bright
Litter of birdcalls strewed the same
Bone-riddled ground. And up the paths
The endless altered people came,

Washing at their identity.
Now, helpless in the hollow of
An unarmorial age, a trough
Of smoke in slow suspended skeins
Above their scrap of history,
Only an attitude remains:

Time has transfigured them into
Untruth. The stone fidelity
They hardly meant has come to be
Their final blazon, and to prove
Our almost-instinct almost true:
What will survive of us is love.

PHILIP LARKIN

Remembrance

Cold in the earth – and the deep snow piled above thee,
Far, far removed, cold in the dreary grave!
Have I forgot, my only Love, to love thee,
Severed at last by Time's all-severing wave?

Now, when alone, do my thoughts no longer hover
Over the mountains, on that northern shore,
Resting their wings where heath and fern-leaves cover
Thy noble heart for ever, ever more?

Cold in the earth – and fifteen wild Decembers
From those brown hills have melted into spring –
Faithful indeed is the spirit that remembers
After such years of change and suffering!

Sweet Love of youth, forgive if I forget thee
While the world's tide is bearing me along:
Other desires and other hopes beset me,
Hopes which obscure, but cannot do thee wrong!

No later light has lightened up my heaven;
No second morn has ever shone for me:
All my life's bliss from thy dear life was given –
All my life's bliss is in the grave with thee.

But, when the days of golden dreams had perished,
And even Despair was powerless to destroy,
Then did I learn how existence could be cherished,
Strengthened, and fed without the aid of joy;

Then did I check the tears of useless passion,
Weaned my young soul from yearning after thine;
Sternly denied its burning wish to hasten
Down to that tomb already more than mine!

And, even yet, I dare not let it languish,
Dare not indulge in Memory's rapturous pain;
Once drinking deep of that divinest anguish,
How could I seek the empty world again?

EMILY BRONTË

Remember

Remember me when I am gone away,
    Gone far away into the silent land;
    When you can no more hold me by the hand,
Nor I half turn to go yet turning stay.
Remember me when no more day by day
    You tell me of our future that you planned:
    Only remember me; you understand
It will be late to counsel then or pray.
Yet if you should forget me for a while
    And afterwards remember, do not grieve:
    For if the darkness and corruption leave
    A vestige of the thoughts that once I had,
Better by far you should forget and smile
    Than that you should remember and be sad.

CHRISTINA ROSSETTI

Index of Poets

181

Index of First Lines

Never seek to tell thy love   138
None ever was in love with me but grief.   148
Not easy to state the change you made.   12
Now sleeps the crimson petal, now the white;   52

O lady, when the tipped cup of the moon blessed you   143
O mistress mine, where are you roaming?   69
O, my luve's like a red, red rose,   14
O my thoughts' sweet food, my my only owner,   108
O rose, thou art sick!   130
O sweetheart, hear you   49
O, we loved long and happily, God knows!   153
O western wind, when wilt thou blow   158
Oh, she walked unaware of her own increasing beauty   146
Oh, when I was in love with you,   150
Once, as a child, I ate raspberries. And forgot.   166
One minute I had the windows open   112
One word is too often profaned   5
Our love was conceived in silence and must live silently.   88
Out upon it, I have loved   74

Presage and caveat not only seem   131

Remember me when I am gone away,   180

Shall I come, sweet Love, to thee,   29
She came in from the snowing air   27
She dwelt among the untrodden ways   168
She is as in a field a silken tent   47
She stood breast high amid the corn,   50
She tells her love while half asleep   56
She walks in beauty, like the night   46
Side by side, their faces blurred,   176
So smooth, so sweet, so silvery, is thy voice   24
So we must say Goodbye, my darling,   62
So well I love thee as without thee I   95
Stand on the highest pavement of the stair –   132
Surprised by joy – impatient as the wind   169

Take of me what is not my own,   114
The grey sea and the long black land;   36
The half-moon westers low, my love,   158
The light in the window seemed perpetual   89